Mary DeMuth

PRAY EVERY DAY

HARVEST HOUSE PUBLISHERS
EUGENE, OREGON

Cover by Emily Weigel Design

Cover photo © Rosapompelmo / Shutterstock

Mary E. DeMuth is represented by David Van Diest from the Van Diest Literary Agency, 34947 SE Brooks Road, Boring, OR 97009.

Pray Every Day
Copyright © 2020 by Mary DeMuth
Published by Harvest House Publishers
Eugene, Oregon 97408
www.harvesthousepublishers.com

ISBN 978-0-7369-8009-8 (pbk.)
ISBN 978-0-7369-8010-4 (eBook)

Names: DeMuth, Mary E., - author.
Title: Pray every day : 90 days of prayer from God's word / Mary E DeMuth.
Description: Eugene, Oregon : Harvest House Publishers, [2020] | Summary:
   "Mary DeMuth new devotional Pray Every Day unpacks 90 of the most
   timeless prayers recorded in both the Old and New Testaments and
   explores Scripture's instructions on prayer through daily readings and
   prayer prompts"-- Provided by publisher.
Identifiers: LCCN 2019060180 (print) | LCCN 2019060181 (ebook) | ISBN
   9780736980098 (paperback) | ISBN 9780736980104 (ebook)
Subjects: LCSH: Bible--Prayers--History and criticism. | Bible--Devotional
   use. | Prayer--Christianity.
Classification: LCC BS680.P64 D45 2020 (print) | LCC BS680.P64 (ebook) |
   DDC 242/.5--dc23
LC record available at https://lccn.loc.gov/2019060180
LC ebook record available at https://lccn.loc.gov/2019060181

Printed in the United States of America

20 21 22 23 24 25 26 27 28 / VP-GL / 10 9 8 7 6 5 4 3 2 1

To Holly Schmidt, who loves to pray and lives for Jesus.

CONTENTS

INTRODUCTION

This book began several years ago because I love to pray for others. In my monthly e-zine, I end each letter with "Mind if I pray for you?" And then I pray for the folks receiving the email. Over the years, people have contacted me in several ways—via email, in person, and through the mail—asking me to write a book of my prayers. I created a proposal and shopped it for a few years to no takers. But once I gave it to Harvest House, they saw the project's merits and published *Jesus Every Day*, a 365-day devotional that empowers readers to pray through Scripture from Genesis to Revelation.

When the book released, I had a fortuitous retreat with my mastermind group—a group of Christ-following authors. During our time there, each of us took the hot seat, where we would share a conundrum. I shared, "I would like to promote *Jesus Every Day* in a unique way." My group of friends suggested I start a podcast. I could call it *Pray Every Day*, my friend Thomas suggested. Following the same pattern of the book, I could read through Scripture, then pray it for my audience.

I launched the podcast in February 2018. My heart in doing so was to pray for the world. As of this writing, the podcast has reached more than 100 countries and has been downloaded hundreds of thousands of times. God has expanded this prayer ministry in ways I could not imagine. Thanks to help from others, *Pray Every Day* now has an app on iTunes and Google Play, and you can even access it on your Alexa device.

Imagine my joy when I hear from listeners all over the world!

Anna from Hungary wrote, "I got an Amazon Echo for Christmas, and I was curious if it could help boost my spiritual life somehow.

That's how I found *Pray Every Day.* Listening to it is part of my morning routine now, and it's so good! So thank you."

Jimena from Colombia shared, "I'm 30, and I've been a Christian all my life through my parents, but two years ago I was baptized. I love your podcast, and I hear it every single day. I was searching for Christian podcasts, and I came across yours and some others, and it has become my morning routine. Thank you for giving us some daily inspiration in the Lord!"

Jessica from the United States emailed me this: "Mary, I just wanted to let you know that I felt like your prayer on the podcast this morning was meant for me. I am a caregiver by trade, and sometimes I need to be reminded that it really is a ministry. I also have trouble speaking up and have been getting discouraged regarding what I have felt God is calling me to do. Your prayer greatly encouraged me, and I pray for you, too, as I know you have opposition and attacks come against you. Thank you so much for your ministry."

This broken world we live in needs prayer. I need prayer. You need prayer.

As a continuation of the *Pray Every Day* podcast, I thought it would be interesting to look at 90 prayers from the Bible. As I uncovered these prayers, I was moved, challenged, and changed. In studying those who prayed in Scripture, I saw a swath of humanity as wide as the Mediterranean Sea: a patriarch, a disgraced murderer, one who formed a golden calf, the least in his clan, a childless woman, a shepherd king and his son, a wall builder, a righteous man who suffered the crushing blow of loss, an unknown psalmist, the weeping prophet, an exile in a foreign land, sailors on a sinking boat, a reluctant prophet, Jesus himself, lepers, officials, disciples, men and women longing for healing (for themselves and their loved ones), the blind, a denier of Jesus, one whose face shone during martyrdom, a church persecutor, elders, and angels. What does this tell us about prayer? God offers everyone this extraordinary gift. And you can access that line of communication with him at any moment—even as you're reading this text.

What a privilege it is to build our relationship with God through prayer—to honestly share our hearts with the One who perplexes us, saves our souls, created the universe with a word, and is the author and finisher of our faith. We don't have to use high language. There is no need to impress. In fact, the essential ingredient in coming to him is humility, acknowledging he is God and we are not. He is the Creator; we are the created. And yet, this Creator made a way for us to stay close to him. Through the life, death, and resurrection of Jesus Christ, the Son of God, we have unfettered access to the holy of holies. At any given moment, whether we are crying out in pain, rejoicing in hope, or suffering unjustly, we can approach the throne of grace with confidence (Hebrews 4:16).

One of the passages on prayer I didn't highlight in the following 90 devotions comes from the book of James. The Lord's brother asks,

> Are any of you suffering hardships? You should pray. Are any of you happy? You should sing praises. Are any of you sick? You should call for the elders of the church to come and pray over you, anointing you with oil in the name of the Lord. Such a prayer offered in faith will heal the sick, and the Lord will make you well. And if you have committed any sins, you will be forgiven (James 5:13-15).

Whether broken, joyful, or sick, our task is to pray. Recently, my husband and I accompanied our dear friend who had been diagnosed with aggressive cancer as she went to be prayed for by the elders of our church. They anointed her with oil and prayed over her, while many of us cried out in hope. Though impossible, she is with us today—still battling cancer, but defying the odds.

I understand that people don't always receive the answer they want in prayer. (One of my dear friends lost her cancer battle four years ago, and I still grieve.) The point of prayer is not merely to list our requests, but to press into knowing Jesus better. As the elders, my husband, and I prayed for my friend, we all experienced him in a profound way.

This type of prayer indicates its communal importance. James continues,

> Confess your sins to each other and pray for each other so that you may be healed. The earnest prayer of a righteous person has great power and produces wonderful results. Elijah was as human as we are, and yet when he prayed earnestly that no rain would fall, none fell for three and a half years! Then, when he prayed again, the sky sent down rain and the earth began to yield its crops (James 5:16-18).

We can confess our sins to one another, experiencing profound release as someone else hears our struggle (and it is no longer torturing us in the darkness). As people of prayer, we have the privilege, too, of asking for supernatural intervention as Elijah did.

My prayer for you as you work your way through the next 90 days is that you will experience God in a profound, life-changing way. It's my hope that you'll discover the beauty and power of prayer, and that you will walk through a prolonged deepening of your relationship with God. You'll find every sort of prayer in this devotional—from hollers of lament to praises of gratitude, from fear for the future to faith for the sake of others, from cries of grief to hope for unity. I hope every shadow and nuance of prayer will touch you as you face every circumstance. And I pray you'll close this book as a different person.

Mind if I pray for you?

Jesus, I pray for my friend reading this devotional, that each day will touch them in a specific, *them*-shaped way. Bring clarity in muddied thought. Bring hope where helplessness rules. Bring light when darkness threatens the horizon. Speak truth over every conundrum. Infuse them with righteousness and justice. Sing lovingly over their lives. Empower them to walk in strength and dignity. Replace fear with faith. Heal them of deep emotional wounds. Restore their joy in salvation. Usher in physical healing. Empower them to let go of bitterness and vengeance. Clean their hearts, minds, and souls in a profound way. Reveal what's next. Bring life to their relationships, reconciliation with enemies, and the return of the prodigals in their lives. May they pray every day, experiencing your delight. Amen.

DAY ONE

ABRAHAM

Abraham said to God,
"May Ishmael live under your special blessing!"

GENESIS 17:18

This prayer shows us the longing of a father's heart for his son, aching to see his offspring blessed by the God who bestows kindness and favor on his children. This is the cry of one who hopes the best for another. This desire for a blessing expresses a universal, unconstrained need. Abraham's words are instructive to us today and can deeply empower our prayer lives.

So as we begin this journey of praying through the Bible, let's start with blessing. Think of someone in your life who is struggling with knowing that God is the One who blesses. Pray this over a family member who needs second-chance grace, the kind of grace that pursues those who are far from God—or pray this for a friend who cannot see light in the darkness.

The Hebrew translation of this prayer augments the word *blessing*. It's a series of words that mean "that Ishmael might live before [God]." [1] And the blessing involves Ishmael's face, that he would experience God as he faced the Almighty. There is relationship coursing through this verse, depicting the God who lovingly faces his creation, who walks behind, before, and beside as a protective parent. That is the essence of the blessings we pray over our loved ones—that God would shine his face upon those who need him, and that he would protect, defend, and be with his children.

It is much more difficult to pray a blessing upon someone with whom you're in conflict. Part of your healing journey may be asking this for your friend or a family member who perplexes you: *Lord, I pray they would live before you, that you would prosper their soul.* In praying for our painful relationships, we become more like Jesus.

To pray for another is to bless them—to dare to ask that the One who made every heart, body, and soul would protect and walk gloriously alongside them. We see this in beautiful fulfillment as Jesus incarnates God on earth, facing the creation he fashioned, showing us the heart of the One who blesses us all.

We are blessed so that we can bless. We are given grace so that we can give grace to others. We are loved so that we can embody love to someone who truly needs it. We are forgiven so that we can learn the art and joy of forgiving another.

Jesus, would you bless the person I'm thinking of right now? Would you walk alongside them, bring comfort, show them that you see them? Would you turn their face toward yours? Would you reveal yourself to be faithful, utterly reliable, and wholly interested in their welfare? I entrust them to you. Amen.

DAY TWO

JACOB

Jacob made this vow: "If God will indeed be with me and protect me on this journey, and if he will provide me with food and clothing, and if I return safely to my father's home, then the LORD will certainly be my God. And this memorial pillar I have set up will become a place for worshiping God, and I will present to God a tenth of everything he gives me."

GENESIS 28:20-22

Jacob is the patron saint of the doubter. He throws three ifs toward God in this vow and only promises allegiance when God meets all three conditions. Jacob did not have the privilege we have of reading his story from beginning to end. As he states these many ifs, he is *in medias res*, a storytelling term that simply means he is in the middle of a journey. This passage is a snapshot of Jacob in doubt.

That should bring us deep comfort because we, too, live the life of faith in the middle of our journey, without known outcomes to light our way. We understand from Hebrews 11:1 that "faith shows the reality of what we hope for; it is the evidence of things we cannot see." Jacob could not know that his was the lineage of Israel, that the blessing of God would flow through him, the second-born twin of trickery. He is proof that even connivers and scoundrels can find favor and comfort.

Jacob asks for protection, provision, and position in this prayer—to be protected from harm, to be provided food and clothing, and to be positioned back in his homeland. He echoes the Lord's Prayer:

Our Father in heaven, may your name be kept holy. May your Kingdom come soon. May your will be done on earth, as it is in heaven. Give us today the food we need, and forgive us our sins, as we have forgiven those who sin against us. And don't let us yield to temptation, but rescue us from the evil one (Matthew 6:9-13).

It is good and right for us to ask for these things. Why? Because it shows our reliance on God to provide everything we need. And it invites God into our worries. All of this should end as Jacob ends his vow—in worshipping God for who he is and how extravagantly he loves. We owe him everything, not merely a tenth. Because of his faithfulness, we owe him our very lives.

Jesus, thank you for the vulnerability of Jacob's prayer, that he worried about safety, food, clothing, shelter, and home. Please provide what I need. And as you do so, keep me in a posture of gratitude for all you have done. You are so good. So strong. I choose to worship you with everything within me. Amen.

DAY THREE

Moses

Moses returned to the LORD and said, "Oh, what a terrible sin these people have committed. They have made gods of gold for themselves. But now, if you will only forgive their sin—but if not, erase my name from the record you have written!"

EXODUS 32:31-32

We live in a world where we continually commit the sin of making gods of gold for ourselves, where the pervasive ideology becomes preferring money over what matters. People have sacrificed dignity, relationships, and right living on the altar of consumption. And it is our job to pray for those ensnared by the corrupt mind-set that material possessions and money are all that matters. The almighty dollar-euro-pound-yen-rand is a cheap substitute for the Almighty God.

What a stunningly sacrificial prayer Moses offers here for the money-bent nation of Israel. It echoes the sentiment of the apostle Paul: "My heart is filled with bitter sorrow and unending grief for my people, my Jewish brothers and sisters. I would be willing to be forever cursed—cut off from Christ!—if that would save them" (Romans 9:2-3). Moses's prayer is one of deep intercession, attempting to take upon himself what only Christ could do—to bear the sins of another.

Have you ever experienced this kind of affection toward those for whom you pray? That you feel you would willingly be cut off from Christ so that someone else might experience his grace and glory? This is the cry of love, the prayer of the intercessor, the longing of the one who stands in the gaping hole between a holy God and his unholy people.

Moses prays for God's forgiveness for those who have willingly turned away. We can pray the same, realizing that we, too, willingly turn away. We are clay-footed folks longing for security more than we long for the Savior. Thankfully, we have an advocate in Jesus Christ, who lives to intercede for us day and night. "My dear children, I am writing this to you so that you will not sin. But if anyone does sin, we have an advocate who pleads our case before the Father. He is Jesus Christ, the one who is truly righteous" (1 John 2:1).

Whether we pray for ourselves, trusting in Jesus our advocate, or we intercede for those in our lives who are far from him, we can be reassured that we will never have to experience hell. Jesus faced it all as he died on the cross. He accomplished this prayer, being cut off from the Father, so we would not have to be.

Jesus, how can I thank you for such a sacrifice? I pray for myself and my friends and family who have been wayward. Help us realize that the things of this world will not satisfy. Help me pray all the more fervently for those who are trapped by the trappings of this world. Thank you for going to the cross for me. I cannot adequately express my gratitude. Amen.

DAY FOUR

MOSES

*Moses said, "If you don't personally go with us, don't make us
leave this place. How will anyone know that you look favorably
on me—on me and on your people—if you don't go with us?
For your presence among us sets your people and me apart
from all other people on the earth."*

EXODUS 33:15-16

Moses is known as a man who speaks with God (see Exodus
33:11). This passage comes after an interaction they had where
God promised to walk *only* with Moses, not the nation of Israel. Moses
then intercedes, pleading with God to go with them all. God's response?
"I will indeed do what you have asked, for I look favorably on you, and
I know you by name" (verse 17).

After this discourse, Moses asks the seemingly impossible—to see
God's glorious presence. God acquiesces, telling him he'll let an aspect
of his character, his goodness, pass before Moses. But he will not allow
Moses to see his face, or death will be the result. And as God passes in
front of Moses, God exclaims, "Yahweh! The LORD! The God of compassion and mercy! I am slow to anger and filled with unfailing love
and faithfulness" (Exodus 34:6).

After this powerful encounter, Moses watches as God re-chisels the
Ten Commandments into two great tablets and confirms his covenant
with the nation of Israel.

Perhaps this can serve as a model of prayer for us—intercession,
presence, experience. We intercede for those who are in rebellion. We
ache for them and bring them mightily before the mighty One. We ask

that God would go with our loved ones. And then? We seek his face, his presence, his gaze. We dare to pursue God audaciously, not merely for our requests and intercessions, but simply for an experience of his presence. And then, we wait. On our knees, with hearts bowed to the One who made it all, in holy expectation.

In that space of intercession and interaction, we experience the power of God, not only on our behalf, but on behalf of the wayward. We see echoes of this framework in the way Jesus prays for all of us in John 17:24: "Father, I want these whom you have given me to be with me where I am. Then they can see all the glory you gave me because you loved me even before the world began!" This glory Moses sought is satisfied in Jesus Christ, who made a way for all people to know him.

Face to face is now possible.

Jesus, teach me what it means to truly intercede for those who are far from you. I want them, I long for them, to know and see you face-to-face. Thank you that you made a way for me to experience your glorious presence. I don't take it for granted. I don't treat it nonchalantly. I hunger more and more for you. May it be that my friends and family who are far from you do the same. Amen.

DAY FIVE

AARON

*May the LORD bless you and protect you. May the LORD
smile on you and be gracious to you. May the LORD show
you his favor and give you his peace.*

NUMBERS 6:24-26

This is what we long for, isn't it? Blessing, protection, smiles, grace, favor, peace. How beautifully this blessing echoes the fruits of the Spirit in Galatians 5:22-23: "The Holy Spirit produces this kind of fruit in our lives: love, joy, peace, patience, kindness, goodness, faithfulness, gentleness, and self-control. There is no law against these things!" Moses represents the law, but here we have sheer grace in gifts doled out by the Holy Spirit. This is our inheritance as believers in Jesus Christ.

These traits can be manufactured by others, but they are only genuinely experienced through the presence of God, whose character emits them. The name for God here is Yahweh, the ever-existing One, the great I Am. Perhaps a better reading of this passage is this:

Because God is full of blessings and protection, he will protect.

Because God has a joyful countenance, he will smile upon you.

Because God is grace personified, he will offer that grace in abundance.

Because God is the source of favor, he will call you his favored one.

Because God is shalom (peace), he will grant that to you in wide measure.

He is, so we will be.

He gives from who he is.

Let today be the day you proclaim these blessings over your loved ones because of God's faithfulness. This is concrete work, based on the fact of his goodness and nature. It is not wishful thinking or misplaced hope. No, as you bless your loved ones, you are relying on the One who created them in the first place. You are demonstrating your trust in the unhindered nature of God Almighty, who lavishes love and grace on generations of people. You are walking in the truth that life comes from the Author of life.

So bless the people in your life. See them as God sees them—as those for whom he protects, shines his face, offers abundant grace, favors lavishly, and grants the elusive peace for which the world clamors.

Jesus, I bless those who so desperately need to know your goodness. Thank you that your blessings upon others flow from your unchangeable nature. You are their protector. Please smile upon them today, offering grace, favor, and peace. Help me see them as you do, Lord. Transform my heart toward them. Amen.

DAY SIX

MOSES

I can't carry all these people by myself! The load is far too heavy!
If this is how you intend to treat me, just go ahead and kill me.
Do me a favor and spare me this misery!

NUMBERS 11:14-15

Prayer is meant to be honest. It's a frank conversation about our actual lives in this very moment delivered to a God who sometimes appears unconcerned with our day-to-day struggles. In this prayer, Moses expresses that he has had enough. He is weary, overworked, and railroaded by the people of God. Aggravated and exhausted, Moses holds nothing back from God. He asks very normal questions, questions we ask as well:

- Why did this happen?
- Why do people hurt me?
- How can I carry this unrelenting burden when it crushes my resolve?
- How can I provide for my family?
- Why can't you take my life?
- How long do I have to endure this trial?

What Moses is longing for is to be seen by the One who created him. He needs to know that the God who created everything—in a vast, beautiful cacophony of creativity—takes notice of the small. Yes, he made the planets and plants, but he also made those who plant, and he loves all those who bear his image.

If we studied this prayer without context, we'd think God didn't care about Moses and his plight. But if we flip forward to Numbers 12, we see a God who is deeply concerned with Moses, particularly when it comes to people whining and complaining against him, destroying his authority and resolve. He experienced criticism not merely from the crowds, but from the lips of Miriam and Aaron, those closest to him.

God called them into the tabernacle and said these words in response: "If there were prophets among you, I, the LORD, would reveal myself in visions. I would speak to them in dreams. But not with my servant Moses. Of all my house, he is the one I trust. I speak to him face to face, clearly, and not in riddles! He sees the LORD as he is. So why were you not afraid to criticize my servant Moses?" (verses 6-8).

God did answer Moses's complaint—openly and powerfully. Why? Because God considered Moses trustworthy. They walked together in relationship, talking face-to-face. Moses had a clear picture of who God was. As we pray, we must consider whether or not *we* are trustworthy. Can God entrust us with his secrets? Do we long to spend time with him as a companion and friend? Do we truly chase him?

> God of heaven, Lord of earth, I want to be trustworthy. I want to know you as a friend—no pretense, no playacting. I need to know you are working on my behalf even when I'm exhausted and overburdened. I pray for respite today. But more than that, I simply want to know you are with me. Hold me, please. Amen.

DAY SEVEN

MOSES

*The people came to Moses and cried out, "We have sinned by
speaking against the LORD and against you. Pray that the LORD
will take away the snakes." So Moses prayed for the people.*

NUMBERS 21:7

There are different kinds of prayers throughout the Bible. This one
is clearly intercession, asking on behalf of another. While Moses
prayed that literal snakes would go away, we can also look at this type of
prayer metaphorically. We intercede for people who are far from God
because of their rebellion. In this verse, the Israelites confessed their
sins, then begged Moses to intervene on their behalf.

We, too, can pray to the Lord, asking that he would recognize
the repentance of others and have mercy on them as they walk
through the consequences of their behavior. This is good and important
work, the kind of battle we fight on our knees in the place of others.

Throughout the Old Testament we see circumstances, people, and
stories pointing toward the future. We see echoes, shadows, and hints
of Jesus, who is to come. In this passage, we see the people of God asking someone else to do their praying for them. Their grief and shame
are so great, they long for a more holy intermediary to beckon God on
their behalf—Moses.

For us today, Jesus is that perfect intermediary. He is the most holy
One who not only sits at the right hand of the throne of God, interceding for his children, but who also shed his blood on the cross as a
perfect sacrifice for our sins. And if we look backward toward Genesis,

we see even more clearly what he did in terms of fulfilling prophecy. God tells the serpent of old who incited Adam and Eve to sin, "I will cause hostility between you and the woman, and between your offspring and her offspring. He will strike your head, and you will strike his heel" (Genesis 3:15).

See how this passage beautifully shares the gospel? Sin entered the world through Satan and human rebellion. Consequences reigned. The snake seemed to have won. But Jesus struck Satan's head as he died and rose again, forever living to intercede for us. Next time you pray for your wayward friend, keep this powerful truth in mind.

Jesus, I pray for my loved one who is suffering from the consequences of their behavior. I pray they would continue to choose the hard road of repentance. I pray they will understand what you have done on their behalf, that you've conquered Satan—the serpent of old—and you will empower them to seek you anew. Amen.

DAY EIGHT

MOSES

I prayed to the LORD and said, "O Sovereign LORD, do not destroy them. They are your own people. They are your special possession, whom you redeemed from Egypt by your mighty power and your strong hand. Please overlook the stubbornness and the awful sin of these people, and remember instead your servants Abraham, Isaac, and Jacob."

DEUTERONOMY 9:26-27

M oses prays to the Sovereign LORD. The word *sovereign* here is the Hebrew word *adonai*, which means master, king, and superiority. The small caps represented here simply means that he is praying to Jehovah, "the existing One." [2] We, too, can have utter confidence as we pray to the One who is superior over everything, who reigns and rules over his creation. When life seems to spiral out of control, we can find solace in the truth that the God who created everything we see is in control.

In this prayer, Moses reminds God of his creation. God created the people of Israel as his "special possession." Their mission was to reflect the glory and beauty of God to the entire world. Sadly, the nation often chose rebellion over reflection. Mired in their sin nature and in desperate need of a savior, they continually failed to live out their calling.

In a very real way, these people for whom Moses interceded are like our friends and family members who don't yet know Jesus Christ. Without the Holy Spirit within them, they, too, are enslaved to sin, in need of the Savior. To pray for our lost loved ones is to realize afresh that Jesus is the only way they will ever be freed.

Moses persevered in prayer for the rebellious, and we should too. Because of Jesus Christ, his outrageous grace on the cross and his life-altering resurrection, those who are far from him can be brought near through his blood. He personified Moses's prayer as the One with mighty power and a strong hand. He is the deliverer of all, not merely saving Israelites from seen enemies, but also rescuing us from the enemy of our souls. He is the sovereign, existing One who takes away the rebellion of the world. This is good news.

Jesus, I pray for those who are reveling in active rebellion right now. Please rescue them from themselves. Seek them out. I am grateful that you have provided a way for them to find rescue. Would you give them the inclination to want to be saved? I pray this fervently in your name. Amen.

DAY NINE

JOSHUA

On the day the LORD gave the Israelites victory over the Amorites, Joshua prayed to the LORD in front of all the people of Israel. He said, "Let the sun stand still over Gibeon, and the moon over the valley of Aijalon." So the sun stood still and the moon stayed in place until the nation of Israel had defeated its enemies. Is this event not recorded in The Book of Jashar? *The sun stayed in the middle of the sky, and it did not set as on a normal day. There has never been a day like this one before or since, when the LORD answered such a prayer. Surely the LORD fought for Israel that day!*

JOSHUA 10:12-14

I t's important we digest verse 14 as we consider this passage. "There has never been a day like this" when the sun stood still in light of the prayer of one man. This shows us that we serve a creative and powerful God who controls the cosmos. He can do whatever he pleases, and it pleases him to answer the prayers of his servants.

And what an audacious prayer! Said in public, no less. Joshua might have heard from the Lord prior to this prayer, knowing that God would display his power, but we are not told in the text. We *are* told that immediately preceding this prayer, God fought for the Israelite army by sending large hailstones from the sky upon their enemies. This, perhaps, emboldened Joshua's plea.

Likewise, we can grow in our knowledge of God's power on our behalf as we come closer to him. And as we experience the goodness and power of God, our prayers will become bolder. When we see his goodness as we reflect on the past, we begin to see his trustworthiness, which means that every single day we can become more audacious in our prayers for this world and our lives. Once we've seen God fight for us and then recount it as remembrance, we can boldly fight for others on our knees, entrusting ourselves to the One who rescues.

Rest today in knowing that the God who holds the sun, moon, and stars in his hands holds you close. The One who can defy the laws of physics is powerfully able to come to your side. He fights for you. He sees the battle you fight today. And he loves to intervene for those who pray bold prayers.

Jesus, it's hard for me to understand that you hold everything in your hands, and that all things hold together in you. Help me remember just how powerful you are, particularly when I pray for the incidents in my life that don't seem to improve. I choose to trust you today in the midst of my circumstances. Amen.

DAY TEN

GIDEON

*The LORD turned to him and said, "Go with the strength you
have, and rescue Israel from the Midianites. I am sending
you!" "But Lord," Gideon replied, "how can I rescue Israel?
My clan is the weakest in the whole tribe of Manasseh, and
I am the least in my entire family!" The LORD said to him,
"I will be with you. And you will destroy the Midianites
as if you were fighting against one man."*

JUDGES 6:14-16

Gideon has a conversation with God in this passage—the God
who encourages Gideon to use the strength he already has. God
promises Gideon that he is sending him into the battle and implies that
he will deliver Gideon and his men from the Midianites—as if Gideon
is fighting one man, not an army of men. Following this interaction, we
see Gideon double-making-sure that God would be with him by using
a fleece to determine if God would fulfill his promise of deliverance.

In this passage, we see why he relies on the fleece. He feels utterly
small. Of the important people in Israel, he is found wanting. He is
not the best choice; in fact, he feels he is the exact opposite of best. He
is the least. Have you ever felt this way?

It's interesting to note that God does not rebuke Gideon for his
perceived frailty. He simply reminds Gideon that he will be with him.
God's presence is what is great, and that greatness is best met with weakness. We see this beautiful conundrum throughout the Bible: God's
"strength is made perfect in weakness" (2 Corinthians 12:9 NKJV).

Sometimes we feel we have to be powerful to be heard by a powerful

God. But the opposite is true. God chases those who know their weakness, causing them to reach for his strength. If we gloried in our own strength, we'd be guilty of the sin of pride, and our hearts would be too puffed up to welcome God inside.

You may be like Gideon today, shaking in your boots, worried about many things, afraid of the battle raging outside your door. But the good news is this: God sees you. He hears you. And he invites you to be honest with him. He already knows what you're feeling and thinking, so why not, like Gideon, share your heart with him? In that place of honesty, you'll find new levels of his strength.

Jesus, I don't feel strong or magnanimous or powerful. In fact, I feel small, less than. In this place of honesty, would you meet me here? I am grateful that your strength is made more perfect on the stage of my weakness. Empower me today to face the battle raging outside my prayer closet. Amen.

DAY ELEVEN

JEPHTHAH

*Jephthah made a vow to the LORD. He said, "If you give me
victory over the Ammonites, I will give to the LORD whatever
comes out of my house to meet me when I return in triumph.
I will sacrifice it as a burnt offering."*

JUDGES 11:30-31

Be careful what you declare in prayer. Making a vow before God is
not something one should do flippantly. A vow should be carefully thought out, as we will see in a couple days with the narrative of
Hannah. In the next section of Judges 11, we see the consequences of
Jephthah's hasty declaration. It is his daughter who comes out of his
house, dancing (verse 34).

Jesus spoke of vows quite pointedly:

> I say, do not make any vows! Do not say, "By heaven!"
> because heaven is God's throne. And do not say, "By the
> earth!" because the earth is his footstool. And do not say,
> "By Jerusalem!" for Jerusalem is the city of the great King.
> Do not even say, "By my head!" for you can't turn one hair
> white or black. Just say a simple, "Yes, I will," or "No, I
> won't." Anything beyond this is from the evil one (Matthew 5:34-37).

Another translation puts it this way: "Let your 'Yes' be 'Yes,' and
your 'No,' 'No'" (verse 37 NKJV).

Why does Jesus say this? Because vows are often made in emotionally charged situations, and our words may not reflect logical thinking. We may regret those vows when the emotion is gone. He also says this because our words have meaning, and if we say we vow to do something, we are obligated to do what we say.

What does this have to do with prayer? Simply this: When we are desperate, we may make vows to God as we speak to him. Who hasn't heard of folks facing death or severe consequences saying things like, "I will never drink again if you get me out of this mess"? Or people might promise to live perfect lives if God will heal them of cancer or other terrible maladies.

Vows make prayer into a commodity—an exchange of "if you do this, I will do that"—when, in fact, prayer is a relationship. It's not a place to make emotional and hasty declarations to the mighty One (as in the case of Jephthah), nor is it a bargaining chip or an assertion of your ability to do something you say you'll do.

Prayer is simply spending time with the God of the universe who loves you, understands your torment and worry, and wants to walk alongside you. Vows and declarations do not represent healthy relationship. They are the mark of either pride or insecurity.

Jesus, teach me to be wise in my words as I pray and as I live. Let my *yes* be *yes* and my *no* be *no* today. I don't want to strike bargains with you in desperation for your help. That is a misunderstanding of your lovingkindness. Thank you that you love and help me despite my wayward heart, that you understand my weakness and long to pour your life into me. Amen.

DAY TWELVE

MANOAH

Manoah prayed to the LORD, saying, "Lord, please let the man
of God come back to us again and give us more instructions
about this son who is to be born." God answered Manoah's
prayer, and the angel of God appeared once again to his wife
as she was sitting in the field.

JUDGES 13:8-9

The name Manoah means rest or quiet, but this scene from the book of Judges is neither restful nor quiet. This man had a radical encounter with God, who took pity on him and his barren wife. His prayer in response is instructive. He asks for further clarification from the Lord about the promise the Lord gave that they would have a son.

This son would turn out to be Samson—a warrior of a man, a hero of Israel who also battled his own demons. He was to be a Nazirite, one who does not drink wine or cut his hair. All these specific instructions came through the angel of the Lord.

Seeking God for insight into our current situations is normal and warranted. It shows our dependence on his wisdom. After all, he created us. He knows us better than we know ourselves, and he is not time bound. He sees behind, beside, and ahead. It is good to ask God for insight about what to do next, particularly if our motive is to honor him.

In the book of James, we see this kind of prayer heralded. "If you need wisdom, ask our generous God, and he will give it to you. He will not rebuke you for asking" (1:5). Our God loves to answer a prayer for wisdom and insight. In the case of Manoah and his wife, he gently prepared them for what would come in Samson's life. He did not rebuke Manoah's request, as if Manoah were bothering him with something trivial.

Throughout the book of Proverbs we see wisdom personified. Wisdom was with God when he created the universe. Blessed are those who seek it with all their heart as if it were a jewel. To ask God for it is to say you are in need, that he is God and you are not. In that space of dependent relationship, you open your heart to hear from God in specific, tangible ways.

Jesus, thank you that I don't have to figure out life on my own. I can ask you for help when I need wisdom. Thank you that you welcome such prayers. Today I ask that you provide the insight I need to make the next good decision. I wait on you. I trust in you. I am grateful for you. Amen.

DAY THIRTEEN

HANNAH

*She made this vow: "O LORD of Heaven's Armies, if you will
look upon my sorrow and answer my prayer and give me a
son, then I will give him back to you. He will be yours for his
entire lifetime, and as a sign that he has been dedicated to
the LORD, his hair will never be cut."*

1 SAMUEL 1:11

Hannah weeps this prayer. In a culture where childlessness suggests someone has been forsaken by God, her grief runs deep.
When Eli the priest hears her prayer outside the tabernacle, he cannot
make out her words and declares her drunk. But she responds, "Oh no,
sir...I haven't been drinking wine or anything stronger. But I am very
discouraged, and I was pouring out my heart to the LORD. Don't think
I am a wicked woman! For I have been praying out of great anguish
and sorrow" (1 Samuel 1:15-16).

Eli tells her that her prayer has been granted, and she, who takes
her vow to God seriously, dedicates her son, Samuel, to the Lord as she
promised. This Samuel would become a prophet who would see the
rise of the kingdom of Israel—all from the desperate prayer of a woman
longing for motherhood.

Note to whom Hannah addresses her prayer: the Lord of Heaven's
Armies (also known as the Lord of Hosts, or Yahweh of Angels). She is
calling on the might of God, the power only he possesses. She knows
he commands legions of angels—and yet, as powerful as angelic beings
are, they live in subjugation to the One greater than them.

Hannah's prayer conveys honesty. She tells God what laments

weigh on her heart, and she does so with such conviction and authenticity that Eli mistakes her for being inebriated.

Her prayer also indicates her dedication to the Lord. The gift she seeks from God, if granted, will be offered back in gratitude. She understands that everything, including the opening of a closed womb, comes from God, and any gift he bestows is a gift worth offering back. She lives her life both openhearted and openhanded, honestly sharing her grief, but willing to worship God in whatever answer he gives.

What a beautiful picture of the power and presence of prayer. When we pray, we tell God we are powerless, but he is powerful. And in the midst of that honest declaration, we experience his nearness. He both listens and intercedes. He carries our burdens. He walks with us in our conundrums. Hannah shows us that our most powerful God can also be our most compassionate ally.

Jesus, I choose today to cease sugarcoating my prayers. Instead, I want to be utterly honest, letting you know what perplexes me. I am powerless to solve my problems, but you are powerful. I need your presence as I face today and as I choose to follow you in this difficult world. Lord, I pray you would grant my request, and as you do, I choose to offer every gift you give me back to you as an offering of thanksgiving. Amen.

DAY FOURTEEN

HANNAH

Hannah prayed: "My heart rejoices in the LORD! The LORD
has made me strong. Now I have an answer for my enemies; I
rejoice because you rescued me. No one is holy like the LORD!
There is no one besides you; there is no Rock like our God."

1 SAMUEL 2:1-2

The aftereffect of God's answered prayer is this beautiful declaration before the Lord, witnessed by Eli, when Hannah fulfills
her vow. She exclaims these words as she is giving her son to the aging
priest, which must be sheer agony for her. Still, she persists in praising
the One who opened her womb despite the tears that fall from her eyes.

Earlier she called God the Lord of Heaven's Armies (1 Samuel 1:11),
but here she addresses him simply as Yahweh, the always-existing One.
She has experienced his power, and now she lives in gratitude. She calls
God "holy," which means utterly *other*. God is set apart, completely
different. He cannot help but be good at all times. She expresses her
joy at the uniqueness of God. Though pagan nations surround Israel
in a pantheon of gods and demonic entities, there is only one God, she
declares, and he is solid and sure, like a firm foundation, a rock.

Where else is God called a rock? Throughout the Old and New Testaments. In Deuteronomy 32:4, Moses declares, "He is the Rock; his
deeds are perfect. Everything he does is just and fair. He is a faithful
God who does no wrong; how just and upright he is!" David writes,
"The LORD is my rock, my fortress, and my savior; my God is my rock,
in whom I find protection. He is my shield, the power that saves me,

and my place of safety" (Psalm 18:2). In the New Testament, this imagery helps us see the divine aspect of Christ, as he is the cornerstone, the foundation of the church. "Together, we are his house, built on the foundation of the apostles and the prophets. And the cornerstone is Christ Jesus himself" (Ephesians 2:20).

Hannah knew this foundational truth: God was her stability. He was her strength. He was her source of rescue. She understood his character because of the struggles she walked through. Because of her barrenness, she had the opportunity to experience God in ways others less desperate may not have. This brings us hope, particularly when our trials seem unfair or unrelenting. There is treasure hidden in our despair, and that treasure is our God.

> Jesus, you are my rock. You are my strength. You are my deliverer. You are my source of rescue. Thank you for your holiness. Thank you for listening to me when I am worried or perplexed or in agony. Thank you that you answer prayers. Thank you for seeing me, for hearing me, for noticing me. Oh, how I love and celebrate you, my sure foundation. Amen.

DAY FIFTEEN

DAVID

*David prayed, "O LORD, God of Israel, I have heard that Saul
is planning to come and destroy Keilah because I am here. Will
the leaders of Keilah betray me to him? And will Saul actually
come as I have heard? O LORD, God of Israel, please tell me."
And the LORD said, "He will come." Again David asked,
"Will the leaders of Keilah betray me and my men to Saul?"
And the LORD replied, "Yes, they will betray you."*

1 SAMUEL 23:10-12

Here we see the intimacy between David and the Lord of Israel. David, in the circle of their relationship, cries out to God about his current predicament by using the ephod of Abiathar the priest as a way of connecting to him. Once again, Saul is bent on destroying David, and David battles insecurity about who is surrounding him (the leaders of Keilah). You can hear the fear in his prayer—life and death stand before him.

In God's kindness, he responds, alerting David to the upcoming danger. This gives David the intel he needs to protect himself and his 600 companions. They retreat to the wilderness in the hill country of Ziph to regroup, and although Saul hunts David with strong determination, he does not find him in that place.

We may not stand at the crossroads of life and death. We may not have enemies bent on killing us, but we do have a very real enemy, the accuser of humanity, who wants nothing more than our destruction. So we can pray for protection. We can ask for wisdom. We can seek God for our next steps. God is all-intelligent. He knows all mysteries and is not confined by time constraints. He is able to come to our rescue, and he loves to communicate with us when we face dire situations.

In the New Testament, Jesus declares that his work is to vanquish evil. First John 3:8 reminds us, "The Son of God came to destroy the works of the devil." We do not need to cower in fear. Like David, we may turn to the Lord, who lives to intercede for us, to protect us from the evil one, and to provide a way through our circumstances. Sometimes that way is through a wilderness. Sometimes it's an instantaneous rescue. Sometimes it's his presence in the midst of suffering. But be assured, God hears your pleas and loves to rescue those facing evil.

Jesus, thank you that you came to destroy the works of the evil one. Thank you that you are touched when we are afraid. Thank you that you communicate with us and freely give us wisdom and help when we ask for it. I choose to rest in knowing that you are with me right now. Vanquish evil, please. And bring me peace as I face the darkness. Amen.

DAY SIXTEEN

DAVID

*O LORD of Heaven's Armies, God of Israel, I have been bold
enough to pray this prayer to you because you have revealed all
this to your servant, saying, "I will build a house for you—a
dynasty of kings!" For you are God, O Sovereign LORD. Your
words are truth, and you have promised these good things to
your servant. And now, may it please you to bless the house of
your servant, so that it may continue forever before you. For you
have spoken, and when you grant a blessing to your servant,
O Sovereign LORD, it is an eternal blessing!*

2 SAMUEL 7:27-29

When we pray, it's important that we approach God with reverence. One of the ways we can do this is to say his proper name as we pray. Here King David calls God three names: Lord of Heaven's Armies (*Jehovah Tsaba*), God (*Elohiym*) of Israel, and Sovereign Lord (*Jehovah Adonai*).

When we call on God as the Lord of Heaven's Armies (the Lord of Hosts in other translations), we are reminding ourselves of his kingly rule over all angelic warriors. This is a military title, one of might and power and strength. Not only has God created everything we see, but he commands the greatest army in a cosmic battle over evil and the kingdoms of darkness. What an amazing privilege it is to pray to him this way. This name also expands to mean he is Lord of the sun, moon, and stars—the whole of creation. What an amazing God we call upon!

When we address God as *Elohiym*, we recognize his otherness. He is divine, not human. As the divine One, he rules over the heavens and the earth with power.

Jehovah Adonai is a name that expresses the sovereign rule of our Creator. The second part of this term is a display of reverence, similar to when a subject calls a king "my lord" or "your majesty." So not only does God have kingly rule over everything we see (and everything we do not see), but this trait of his demands our reverence. For those of us who are unfamiliar with a monarchy, it is hard to wrap our minds around this kind of terminology. While Western culture takes a democratic view of government, a king who rules is all-powerful over his nation. There are no checks and balances. He simply has full reign over his dominion.

King David reveres the God who made him, and even though he himself is a king with a kingdom, he knows that his ultimate allegiance falls at the throne of the One who rules it all. He acknowledges that God rules with truth, something we all desperately need in this world full of half-truths and lies.

O Lord of Heaven's Armies, God of Israel, and Sovereign Lord, I trust you as I offer my requests to you. You are the King of my life. You rule everything I see and cannot see. You are King, and I am not. You are God, and I am not. You are Lord, and I am not. That brings me great comfort. I choose today to trust in your truth, not my own. Amen.

DAY SEVENTEEN

SOLOMON

*Now, O LORD my God, you have made me king instead of my
father, David, but I am like a little child who doesn't know his
way around. And here I am in the midst of your own chosen
people, a nation so great and numerous they cannot be counted!
Give me an understanding heart so that I can govern your
people well and know the difference between right and wrong.
For who by himself is able to govern this great people of yours?*

1 KINGS 3:7-9

God offered something to Solomon we dreamed about as kids
when we rubbed a lamp in the hope of awakening a genie—
essentially a guaranteed wish (no need for three!). Solomon could have
asked for anything—unending wealth, fame throughout the earth, victory over every foe, health, a perfectly orchestrated career, amazing relationships. But Solomon asks for none of these things.

He asks, instead, for wisdom—a prayer God loves to answer. He
approaches God with humility, acknowledging that, in himself, he
does not have the capacity to rule the nation of Israel. He needs God's
wisdom, an understanding heart. He longs to know right and wrong,
to be able to judge correctly. He wants to best steward this authority
he's been granted.

God graciously answers his prayer. And because Solomon doesn't
ask for everything the world could give, but instead seeks God's wisdom, God grants Solomon the other peripheral things as well—icing
on the wisdom cake.

We, too, can pray for wisdom. We can ask God to give us a heart and mind of discernment as we try to navigate a difficult and confusing world. We can humble ourselves before our all-wise God, seeking him for the ability to navigate our circumstances.

Like Solomon, we have been entrusted with the people in our lives. We are stewards of ourselves and our relationships. Our beautifully relational God loves to empower us to love our circle of influence well.

Jesus, how I need wisdom! I don't know how to figure out how to live apart from you. Like Solomon, I ask for your help, especially today. I want to love well, understand the times in which I live, and walk with integrity before my friends and family. I acknowledge that you alone are my source of great wisdom. Forgive me for only relying on my wits. I seek your wisdom today instead. Amen.

DAY EIGHTEEN

Elijah

Elijah cried out to the Lord, "O Lord my God, why have you brought tragedy to this widow who has opened her home to me, causing her son to die?" And he stretched himself out over the child three times and cried out to the Lord, "O Lord my God, please let this child's life return to him."

1 Kings 17:20-21

Elijah was a prophet who often saw the power of God intervene in his life. But here we see his humanity as he desperately prays for a widow's son who has passed from life to death. Elijah has the kind of relationship with God that is utterly honest. He does not conceal his bewilderment or his frustration at the circumstances. After all, the widow in this story had taken care of Elijah in the past. This boy is all she has in the world. Why would God allow such a travesty?

It is good and right to cry out to God in honesty. It is not blasphemous to share our hearts authentically with him. He already knows we carry doubts, concerns, and anger. Why not welcome God into our struggle? Why not acknowledge what is going on in our hearts? It is in this space of utter honesty that we experience his presence.

In his desperation, Elijah stretches himself out over the young, dead boy, pleading for God to give the boy his breath back. He understands that God is the Author of life, and only God could create such a miracle. As this story unfolds, we see the boy take in breath, live again, and bless his mother with newfound life.

We need to keep this in mind when we pray—to be both honest and bold. Honest about our pain and bewilderment and the injustice found in this world, but bold enough to believe that God is big—able to create breath from death.

All our desperate prayers will not be answered as Elijah's was. (It's important to remember that the widow and her son eventually succumbed to death, as did Lazarus in the New Testament.) In the next world, in the new heavens and the new earth, all death will be wiped out. All mourning will cease. And every injustice will be righted. We can trust boldly on this earth, remembering the truth found in Hebrews 11—that not all the saints received what they prayed for, but waited expectantly for what would come.

> Jesus, I want to be someone who prays honestly about what is perplexing me. I want to pray bold prayers, believing you can absolutely do the miraculous. Help me hold my expectations in the tension between your capabilities and your sovereign will. I know that someday all will be made right. Empower me to cling to my faith as I wait. Amen.

DAY NINETEEN

Elisha

Elisha prayed, "O Lord, open his eyes and let him see!"
The Lord opened the young man's eyes, and when he
looked up, he saw that the hillside around Elisha was
filled with horses and chariots of fire.

2 Kings 6:17

Elisha was Elijah's mentee. He, too, was a prophet of the nation of Israel who saw many miracles. In this passage, Elisha's servant, who is with him in Dothan, spies the armies of the king of Aram. They have a vast horde of people, complete with horses and chariots that surround the entire city where Elisha and his servant are staying.

The servant asks, "Oh, sir, what will we do now?" (2 Kings 6:15). You can hear the fear in his plea, the helplessness.

Elisha says, "Don't be afraid...For there are more on our side than on theirs!" (verse 16). Then he prays today's prayer.

God powerfully answered, opening the servant's eyes. Yes, Aram's armies numbered many, but the entire hillside held the fiery armies of God, surrounding them all.

God delivered them that day through his mighty hand. As we have learned in past passages, God is the Lord of Heaven's Armies. In our material world, it is easy to take stock of the worries around us, forgetting that much of the battle we fight is unseen. It's against the forces of wickedness in the heavenly realms (see Ephesians 6:12). It is not fought in our own military might, but through the power of God on our behalf. We simply need to pray, "God, open our eyes to see the battle."

He promises this: "You belong to God, my dear children. You have already won a victory over those people, because the Spirit who lives in you is greater than the spirit who lives in the world" (1 John 4:4).

We have a distinct advantage over Elisha. We have the Spirit of God indwelling us. He empowers us, fights on our behalf, and strengthens us when we are weary from the fight. He subjugates all powers beneath himself. He has the victory. He is the One who raised Jesus from the dead (Romans 8:11)! All that power resides within us. We no longer need to live in fear.

Jesus, I'm amazed that although the battle rages, the victory is yours because you are mighty and strong. Open my eyes to see this victory. Thank you for sending your Spirit to work so powerfully within me. I don't want to faint at the battle, but instead have the correct perspective that you are fighting on my behalf. Amen.

DAY TWENTY

HEZEKIAH

*"Remember, O LORD, how I have always been faithful to
you and have served you single-mindedly, always doing what
pleases you." Then he broke down and wept bitterly.*

2 KINGS 20:3

This is Hezekiah's prayer after he becomes "deathly ill" with a boil.
The prophet Isaiah tells him, "This is what the LORD says: Set
your affairs in order, for you are going to die. You will not recover from
this illness" (2 Kings 20:1).

Can you imagine hearing such dire news? Hezekiah's response is
instructive. He is frank with God, reminding God of his faithfulness
to him. Overcome with grief, he weeps. This prayer is laced with both
faith and reality—faith that perhaps God will hear his desperate plea,
and a sense of reality about the situation, evidenced by tears.

Moved by Hezekiah's prayer, God instructs the prophet Isaiah to
return. He is to tell Hezekiah,

> This is what the LORD, the God of your ancestor David,
> says: I have heard your prayer and seen your tears. I will
> heal you, and three days from now you will get out of bed
> and go to the Temple of the LORD. I will add fifteen years to
> your life, and I will rescue you and this city from the king
> of Assyria. I will defend this city for my own honor and for
> the sake of my servant David (verses 5-6).

God hears our prayers. He notes our desperation. He is moved by our need. Our job is simply to be forthcoming and full of faith. The difficulty comes, though, when God chooses not to heal, not to move in the way we have asked. That can be bewildering and confusing. In times like those, we can pray, "Lord, I don't understand why you have chosen not to heal me, but I want to learn everything you have for me in this time of testing." He has the uncanny ability to move in our desperate circumstances.

He doesn't always rescue us from our current turmoil. Although God added 15 years to Hezekiah's life, Hezekiah eventually succumbed to death. And yet, God's plan unfolded. The entire Old Testament, including the history of Israel that bounced between faithfulness and faithlessness, pointed toward a day when a Savior would come, One who would take our sin and sickness upon his sacred body. In Jesus, we have the ultimate intermediary interceding for us day and night before the throne of God. We can honestly entrust our struggles to One like that.

Jesus, I pray for my situation today. Would you look down upon me, see me, and intercede for me? I need help. I need your perspective. I need deliverance. I need health. I am weary and heavy-laden with worries. I have carried this fear far too long. Rescue me. Amen.

DAY TWENTY-ONE

ASA

Asa cried out to the LORD his God, "O LORD, no one but you
can help the powerless against the mighty! Help us, O LORD our
God, for we trust in you alone. It is in your name that we have
come against this vast horde. O LORD, you are our God; do not
let mere men prevail against you!"

2 CHRONICLES 14:11

What a powerful prayer King Asa prayed as he sought God for deliverance from Zerah's Ethiopian army that stood one million strong! We can learn much from the pattern of this prayer.

First, Asa cried out to God. In his distress, he did not turn to pagan idols, or strategies that had worked in the past (pragmatism), or his own strength. No, he knew that the only way out of this painful and frightening situation was to consult God, to plead his cause before the Almighty.

Second, he recognized the power of God in that he recognized his own powerlessness and the powerlessness of mankind against a God who battles and wins. In other words, Asa went to the "top," to the Commander of Heaven's Armies.

Third, in his plea for help, he conveyed his trust. He realized he could not put his faith in any man-created scheme, and only God deserved his utmost trust.

Fourth, he reveled in the power of the name (the character and reputation) of God. It was God's fame on the line in this struggle against evil. And although the horde was comprised of many, God's greatness trumps the mightiest army.

Fifth, he reminded God that the people of Israel were his. They followed him. They staked their lives on him. They loved and needed him.

Last, he stood in faith, believing that God could do the impossible against seemingly impossible odds. We can do the same.

Jesus, thank you for the example of Asa. I want to pray like that, to cry out in honesty, to recognize you for your great power, to trust in your abilities more than my own, to live for your name and fame, to be considered your child, and to stand in faith, believing you will accomplish what concerns me. I lay my burdens before you, entrusting them to you. Amen.

DAY TWENTY-TWO

EZRA

Praise the LORD, the God of our ancestors, who made the king
want to beautify the Temple of the LORD in Jerusalem! And
praise him for demonstrating such unfailing love to me by
honoring me before the king, his council, and all his mighty
nobles! I felt encouraged because the gracious hand of the LORD
my God was on me. And I gathered some of the leaders of
Israel to return with me to Jerusalem.

EZRA 7:27-28

Ezra begins this prayer with praise—another beautiful pattern to follow when we approach God in prayer. When life overwhelms, or people say mean things, or there are too many bills and not enough paycheck, we always have the opportunity to praise God for who he is and how he's been faithful.

Ezra also recognizes the *hesed* of God—his loyal, unfailing love. Sometimes prayer is simply telling God how grateful we are for his love and the loving ways he has pursued us. And when we intercede for others, we can also discern and trace the hand of God in their lives. It's an encouraging practice to seek the story of God over a lifetime, seeing the twists and turns sovereignly shaped by God's hand.

Oh, how gracious our God is when we dare to look back! His care, concern, and power invigorate our hearts. As followers of Jesus Christ, we can see the moment or series of moments we have experienced in coming to him—his gentle wooing, his very real rescue. Our resulting gratefulness informs our loyalty, but it also undergirds our prayer lives. Gratitude is the fuel that ignites our passion in the act of praying.

May today be a day you look back—to see God's pursuit and faithfulness. May that perspective morph into thankfulness for all he has wrought on your behalf: the relationships he has restored, the pain in your heart he has alleviated, the power of his Spirit over the sin you used to struggle with, his very real pursuit of your loved ones, the journey of healing on which he has taken you, the parts of your heart that were broken but are now made whole.

All this is God's sheer gift to you, and your recounting of his good work is just as much prayer as interceding for others is. So recount his goodness back to him and rest in his smile over you.

Jesus, thank you for all you have done for me. As I look back on my life, I can't help but smile at your faithfulness. I am grateful for the journey on which you've taken me so far. Thank you that gratitude toward you can be my prayer for today. Amen.

DAY TWENTY-THREE

NEHEMIAH

"The people you rescued by your great power and strong hand
are your servants. O Lord, please hear my prayer! Listen to the
prayers of those of us who delight in honoring you. Please grant
me success today by making the king favorable to me.
Put it into his heart to be kind to me." In those
days I was the king's cup-bearer.

NEHEMIAH 1:10-11

I f you want to know how to pray powerfully, study the prayers of
Nehemiah. He was a faithful Jewish follower of God who returned
from exile to rebuild the crumbling walls of Jerusalem. He faced seri-
ous threats—politically, socially, and personally—and his response to
those very real dangers was to pray.

In this prayer, he points out God's fidelity to his people, folks Nehemiah calls the servants of God. He asks God to be attentive to his
prayer, and he reminds God of his great delight in honoring God. Oh,
that we could live such lives—to truly delight in seeing the smile of
God upon us, to find joy in bringing him joy.

Nehemiah also recognizes that no human being can supersede
God's sovereign plan, even if that man be a sovereign (a king) himself.
Instead of trying to force his way into the king's graces, he beseeches
the King of kings to steer the king's heart in favor toward Nehemiah.
That act is instructive to us, especially as we pray for those in authority
and the leaders of our nation and world. Ultimately, we do not need to
be afraid, because our great King sits on the only throne that matters,
and that throne is an approachable throne of grace.

The line following Nehemiah's prayer is an interesting addendum. He prayed these bold prayers not as a regular citizen, outside the commonwealth of power, but as the cupbearer to the king. He had prominence. He could have relied on his wits and wisdom to steer the heart of the king, but he chose not to do so. Instead, he prayed.

May it be that we take this example to heart. No matter what our influence is, it is far better to get on our knees, seeking God for wisdom and intervention, than it is to connive a way for change.

Jesus, I trust you to work on my behalf. I am joyfully your servant. I delight in you today. I cannot change the course of history—whether a nation's or my own—so I humbly entrust everything to you. I pray for my leaders, that you would sovereignly steer their hearts. As you do, help me be utterly faithful to you. Amen.

DAY TWENTY-FOUR

NEHEMIAH

I prayed, "Hear us, our God, for we are being mocked. May
their scoffing fall back on their own heads, and may they
themselves become captives in a foreign land! Do not ignore
their guilt. Do not blot out their sins, for they have provoked
you to anger here in front of the builders." At last the wall
was completed to half its height around the entire city, for the
people had worked with enthusiasm.

NEHEMIAH 4:4-6

It's important to understand the context of Nehemiah's desperate prayer. He had been toiling along with the other returned exiles to rebuild the walls of Jerusalem. An enemy named Sanballat said to the workers, "What does this bunch of poor, feeble Jews think they're doing? Do they think they can build the wall in a single day by just offering a few sacrifices? Do they actually think they can make something of stones from a rubbish heap—and charred ones at that?" (Nehemiah 4:2). Sanballat's tone was mocking derision, and those words threatened to sink into the resolve of the builders.

Couple that with this verbal dagger that came next: "Tobiah the Ammonite, who was standing beside him, remarked, 'That stone wall would collapse if even a fox walked along the top of it!'" (verse 3).

Nehemiah's response was not to debate the naysayers or defend himself. It was not to point out the fallacy of the enemies' statements. It was not to become immobilized with fear. No. It was to pray today's prayer.

Note that Nehemiah did not forsake God's justice in his prayer.

He *did* ask for justice to prevail against the enemies. It is not wrong to appeal to the justice of God in our prayers, as long as we understand that we are not the enactors of vengeance. Nehemiah rightly aligned himself with the perfect Judge of the living and the dead, the One who could mete out appropriate consequences.

The result of Nehemiah's defiantly beautiful prayer was a wall-building victory. The wall, which formerly lay in ruins, now rose to half its height on its way to being fully completed. The enemies came to demoralize the builders, but their taunts had the opposite effect—they pushed Nehemiah to pray. May it be that today's enemy-like voices propel us to do the same.

Jesus, take note of those who speak ill against you and your work. Be just. Help me discern when it's time to fight—not against people taunting me, but on my knees. I want to see your work done on this earth, and I understand you are the One bringing the strength to do so. I choose to rest in that today. Amen.

DAY TWENTY-FIVE

NEHEMIAH

I assigned supervisors for the storerooms: Shelemiah the priest, Zadok the scribe, and Pedaiah, one of the Levites. And I appointed Hanan son of Zaccur and grandson of Mattaniah as their assistant. These men had an excellent reputation, and it was their job to make honest distributions to their fellow Levites. Remember this good deed, O my God, and do not forget all that I have faithfully done for the Temple of my God and its services.

NEHEMIAH 13:13-14

It's important to note that Nehemiah was both a worker and a prayer. After the returning exiles erected the wall around Jerusalem, he set out to right any wrongs in the temple of God and its prescribed worship practices. He found people of good reputation to make sure the temple ran smoothly. No doubt he prayed about how to go about this and whom to appoint.

In today's prayer, Nehemiah reminds God of what he has done. It's not that God would have forgotten Nehemiah's deeds, but in reminding God, Nehemiah continues their communication in that intimate circle of two. It's much like a child would say to his father, "Look at this painting I created!" It's an exchange of affection and conviviality.

Our faith is both praxis (acting out) and belief, and this passage powerfully demonstrates both. Nehemiah acted on behalf of God to ensure the people of God would experience him well. He obeyed. His sacrifice was not merely lip service, but action. His "lip service" became his prayer after his obedience.

Act, then pray. Pray, then act. Both are important. To act is to entrust our actions to an active God. To pray is to realize that our own strength cannot accomplish divine purposes.

What is it that God is calling you to do today? What will benefit the bride of Christ, his church? What action can you take that will build up the body? May the aftereffect of your obedience be a connected conversation with the Lord of the universe, who notices your good works as a father proudly displays a child's artwork on the fridge.

Our God both gives us the power to obey and loves us affectionately as his child. Let's choose to live in light of those twin truths today.

> Jesus, show me where you would like me to work. How can I benefit your church today? How can I speak to a societal ill or bring life to a friend who is hurting? Please show me. And thank you that none of my actions go unnoticed. You see me. You love me. You are delighted in me. Because of that outrageous favor, I choose to delight in you. Amen.

DAY TWENTY-SIX

JOB

*Job stood up and tore his robe in grief. Then he shaved his
head and fell to the ground to worship. He said, "I came
naked from my mother's womb, and I will be naked when
I leave. The LORD gave me what I had, and the LORD has
taken it away. Praise the name of the LORD!" In all of this,
Job did not sin by blaming God.*

JOB 1:20-22

What a powerful response to tragedy—a faith-filled recognition of grief and loss. When we're walking through trauma, it helps to read the book of Job. He was known as an upright man who lived righteously. He had a strong family, a good work ethic, and much wealth, which he had accumulated during his tenure on earth.

Satan asked permission to take all this away from Job—and God, in his sovereignty, allowed it. In our sin-tainted world, this kind of tragedy, sadly, is common. Evil people do evil things. Family members suffer. Our health takes a dive. We lose our wherewithal, our purpose, our financial footing.

Job's prayer is our model of response when those terrible turns inevitably knock on our door. We grieve. We tear at our clothing. We figuratively shave our heads in mourning. God did not rebuke Job for such honest actions. These reactions are normative when it comes to trauma. But what he did next is instructive. He grieved, then prayed. He spoke the truth to the Lord. He came into this world without clothes, completely helpless, and whenever he died (which he may have thought would be soon), he would return to the earth naked. He had nothing when he began life, and he would take nothing from this life.

And yet, even after this solemn acknowledgment of the rhythm of life and death in this fallen world, Job made a choice. He chose to praise God in the pain. He chose not to place the blame on God. He chose to recognize God's sovereign hand. Further into the story of Job, he begins to question and make sense of his tragedy, yes. But in his initial reaction, he chose to believe the best of God even when the worst happened to him.

What a blessing to have someone in Scripture to whom we can relate! Job knew tragedy, and yet he walked through that pain with God, even as his friends spouted platitudes and blame. At the end of the book of Job, we see him move from hearing God (when life was good) to seeing God (in the midst of difficult circumstances). That can become our prayer too: that we would see God, even in the turmoil.

Jesus, thank you for your love. Thank you that nothing happens to me outside your sovereign will. I confess that I don't often praise you when circumstances are hard. Sometimes I blame you, if I'm honest. Help me be more like Job, choosing to wrestle, yes, but also to bless you in the way I respond to life's inevitable pitfalls. Amen.

DAY TWENTY-SEVEN

JOB

Job replied to the LORD,
"I am nothing—how could I ever find the answers?
I will cover my mouth with my hand. I have said too much
already. I have nothing more to say."

JOB 40:3-5

Job walked through hell and back, and as he did, he questioned God. He wondered why all these terrible things had happened to him when he was an upright, God-fearing man. Throughout the book of Job, we see his friends casting accusations his way, discouraging him with clichés, and nagging him about his supposed sin.

Eventually, when he'd had enough, he turned his honest ire toward the Almighty, questioning why all this happened.

God answered back, not with statements of his grandeur, but with questions for Job. Whenever someone asks questions, you can be assured they're interested in communing in relationship, because questions welcome interaction. God asked Job where he was when God created everything Job could see, touch, or hear. He asked where Job had been when he laid the foundations of the world or created the leviathan, a sea creature known in the ancient world.

Job's response was to reply, to continue in that conversation with the Almighty God. In that interaction, he clearly saw he was out of his depth. He could not answer any of God's questions.

Sometimes we forget the intelligence of God, that not only is he omnipotent, but he is also omniscient. He is smart, wise, deeply and profoundly intelligent. We cannot win an argument against him, nor can we understand him. He is completely different from us. Job came face-to-face with this reality.

Job embodies the latter wisdom of Solomon in Ecclesiastes 5:2: "Don't make rash promises, and don't be hasty in bringing matters before God. After all, God is in heaven, and you are here on earth. So let your words be few." Solomon understood this, even with all the wisdom God had graciously granted him.

Sometimes the most proper response is to be quiet, and that, in itself, is prayer. It's an acknowledgment that we cannot, God can, and we choose to surrender with faith to whatever his will is. It's an act of faith, this silence—though keeping quiet is not easy, nor does it come naturally. We'd rather make our case.

Jesus, help me keep my words few when I'm confused and frustrated. Help me have the discipline of silence as I walk through my current struggle. I thank you that you are willing to listen, particularly to everything my silence communicates. You are so smart, so amazing, and I trust that you can do good things even in the midst of my silent grief. Amen.

DAY TWENTY-EIGHT
DAVID

O LORD, I have so many enemies; so many are against me.
So many are saying, "God will never rescue him!" But you,
O LORD, are a shield around me; you are my glory, the one who
holds my head high. I cried out to the LORD, and he answered
me from his holy mountain. I lay down and slept, yet I woke up
in safety, for the LORD was watching over me. I am not afraid of
ten thousand enemies who surround me on every side.

PSALM 3:1-6

When David fled his son Absalom, his enemies expanded from pagan nations and kings to the people within his own household. Have you ever felt that way or experienced familial pain like that? It is one thing to have an enemy disparage you, but quite another when it's your family member actively trying to destroy you. David experienced the heartache of this close-to-home betrayal.

His response? To pour out his heart to God in utter honesty. He didn't honey-coat his pleas. No, he told God the truth of his situation. This is encouraging when you internalize the truth that a king in anguish had such a strong relationship with his King that he felt comfortable enough to pour out his heartache. Since that was true for King David, it is utterly true for us as well. We can share our struggles with God in all honesty. In fact, God welcomes such outpourings!

David's prayer also reflects his faith in the God who protects. God shields us from harm. A shield is an integral part of a warrior's armor, and it is meant to deflect arrows from piercing a soldier. So God similarly protects us. (And isn't it beautiful to consider that Jesus Christ

faced the cross unarmored? He was pierced for our sins. He experienced the very hell from which he protects us.)

David tells God he is the One who lifts his head, who takes him out
of the place of despair and gives him sleep even in the midst of a difficult battle. It is right and good to seek God for this kind of help and
rest. Remember, our God never sleeps. He is the Good Shepherd who
keeps watch over his flock by night. He will not forsake us. He will
not abandon us. He will take care of us. Let's thank him for that today.

Jesus, thank you that I can be utterly honest with you about my struggles, fears, and the difficult people who populate my life. Thank you
for being a shield about me, the lifter of my head. Thank you for bleeding for me on the cross. Thank you for watching over me when I am
sleeping. You are a good God, and I need you today. Amen.

DAY TWENTY-NINE

DAVID

*O LORD, how long will you forget me? Forever? How long
will you look the other way? How long must I struggle with
anguish in my soul, with sorrow in my heart every day? How
long will my enemy have the upper hand?...But I trust in your
unfailing love. I will rejoice because you have rescued me.*

PSALM 13:1-2,5

This prayer of David is known as a lament psalm. When you read all of Psalm 13, note the structure: It begins with grief and questioning (verses 1-2), which is followed by a plea for God's kindness and justice to rule in the problem at hand (verses 3-4), which is then followed by an appeal to God's goodness (verses 5-6). After a string of laments, David concludes by offering trust and praise because he has looked back on his life and accounted for the faithfulness of God.

If you are walking through a spiritual wilderness, or if your circumstances have brought you low, consider writing your own lament psalm. Pour out your questions to God. He can handle them. After all, he already knows what is in your heart. He invites you to share your woes and worries because he loves you. He wants to interact with you about your current pain.

As you work through your questions and frustrations with God, allow yourself to be completely candid with him. This helps you not only experience catharsis through truth telling, but it also serves to get the angst from your heart out into the open.

Follow that by appealing to God's inerrant justice. Remind God of the need for just practices on the earth as well as the importance of dealing with those who have harmed others. This is a good request, as it reflects the righteousness of God.

As you conclude your lament, think back on the faithfulness of God over the course of your life. Recount his kindhearted dealings with you. Meditate upon his interventions. Thank him for all he has done in the past and let his good record of loving you well be the impetus for praise. You'll begin a lament in frustrated anger, but you'll finish it with faith-filled adulation.

Jesus, thank you so much for all you have done in my life. Thank you that you allow me to share my fears and worries and anger with you. Thank you that you don't shy away from my honest ramblings about this world. Would you bring justice to my current situation? Would you listen to my plea? I choose to trust that you hear me and are working on my behalf. I love you. Amen.

DAY THIRTY

DAVID

Turn to me and have mercy, for I am alone and in deep distress.
My problems go from bad to worse. Oh, save me from them
all! Feel my pain and see my trouble. Forgive all my sins.
See how many enemies I have and how viciously they hate
me! Protect me! Rescue my life from them! Do not let me be
disgraced, for in you I take refuge. May integrity and honesty
protect me, for I put my hope in you.

PSALM 25:16-21

The book of Psalms is rich with prayers. If you're struggling to voice your angst to the Lord, consider simply reading this psalm to him. It's known as praying Scripture back to the Lord. You can use David's exact words when words fail you.

In this request, David appeals to the mercy of God. He is, once again, deeply authentic with God about his current predicament: He finds himself isolated and stressed-out. Not only that, but his problems seem to be multiplying. He's experiencing pain. He's walking through trouble. He has sinned against God. He is facing strong enemies. He has pushed up against feelings of deep disgrace for what he's experienced at the hands of others. Have you ever felt this way?

While David pours out his heart to God, he tells God that he has chosen to turn his lamenting into action. He chooses to take refuge in God, to allow God to shelter him in the haven of his hands. He has realized, in the midst of his tumult, that only God could carry him through it. This is the posture of the disciple who deeply loves God—that of surrender and humility.

David chooses to put his hope in the only One who will not change. God is bedrock. He is stable. He is that anchor in the stormy harbor, that place of refuge. And in his recognition of God's steadfastness, David also makes an interesting statement: "May integrity and honesty protect me" (Psalm 25:21). His response to God's protection is a declaration of his own desire for innocence. God's protection informs David's obedience.

Sometimes we suffer because we have sinned. Sometimes we suffer because someone else has sinned. And sometimes we have no earthly idea why we suffer. But we always have the choice to make God our refuge, our safe haven, and we always have the opportunity to ask the Spirit within us to sprout integrity and honesty in us.

Jesus, thank you for being my protection, my Savior, my help in time of need. Thank you for anchoring me to the truth. I choose to rest in your rescue, to harbor myself in your protection. Would you empower me today to have integrity so that my insides and outsides match? And would you give me the guts to be honest? I understand this is your work, not mine, though I know my willingness is important. Amen.

DAY THIRTY-ONE

DAVID

Pour out your unfailing love on those who love you;
give justice to those with honest hearts. Don't let the
proud trample me or the wicked push me around.

PSALM 36:10-11

W here would we be without the unfailing affection of the God
we serve? Every breath, every hope, every longing for change
is anchored in the steadfast, ever-present love of God.

But so many of us have a difficult time really understanding the love
of God. We can speak about it to others. We can assure a frustrated
friend that God sees, knows, listens to, and loves them. Sometimes it's
easier to see God's care for others than it is to experience that love for
ourselves. Why is that? Because we know ourselves. We live inside our
thoughts, and those thoughts often assail us—with the knowledge of
our unworthiness, our bent toward sin, our inadequacy.

The good news is this: God's love for us is absolutely *not* dependent
on our actions or thoughts. It is dependent on his consistent character.
And when love is rooted in something that cannot change, we can be
assured of its existence. Yes, even for us.

So, along with the psalmist, we can pray that God's unfailing
(never changing!) love will be abundantly poured out upon us. Part
of that type of prayer involves a longing for justice—for those who are
harmed, including ourselves. It is right to ask that God would reward
our honesty, that he would see our hearts that long to serve him. It is

right to ask for God's justice to be served, particularly when those who act wickedly are prevailing.

When you feel unloved and unlovely, pray.

When you long for justice, pray.

When you are trampled by the words of proud people, pray.

When you are pushed around by those bent toward wickedness, pray.

Jesus, I take this moment to pray, asking you to show me your love. Drown out the angry voices in my head. Please help me know that you see me as I strive, through the Holy Spirit, to walk in this world with integrity. Bring justice—for me, for those who hurt. Bring the proud to their knees. Correct the wicked, even now. Amen.

DAY THIRTY-TWO

DAVID

Have mercy on me, O God, because of your unfailing love.
Because of your great compassion, blot out the stain of my sins.
Wash me clean from my guilt. Purify me from my sin. For I
recognize my rebellion; it haunts me day and night. Against
you, and you alone, have I sinned; I have done what is evil in
your sight. You will be proved right in what you say, and your
judgment against me is just. For I was born a sinner—yes, from
the moment my mother conceived me. But you desire honesty
from the womb, teaching me wisdom even there.

PSALM 51:1-6

King David poured out his heart to God after Nathan the prophet confronted him about his sexual predation, murderous plot, and subsequent cover-up. He was known as a man after the heart of God, but prior to this confession, he lived in agony, keenly aware of his sin, yet keeping it pushed down in the darkness of his soul.

In this declaration, you see pinpricks of light gently forcing their way into David's darkened state.

When he confesses, he appeals to the good-hearted nature of God. He is truly aware of the holiness and justice of God, but as he kneels to pray, it is the compassion of God he addresses. He understands that no man can heal him of his guilt. He cannot fix his heart situation himself. There is literally nowhere to go except to reach heavenward.

This prayer of repentance is a stunning reminder of how to approach God after sin.

Recount the mercy of God.

Recognize you have nowhere else to turn.

Reaffirm God's ability to cleanse every sin stain.

Repent of what you have done, with genuine sadness, telling the exact truth of your offense.

Recall the justness of God, that the way he has always acted is true and firm.

Revisit your fall from grace and acknowledge your propensity for deceit.

Retrace the hand of God on your life from your infancy.

Jesus, I choose today to let you sift through my intentions and actions. I know you are compassionate and full of love, and I appeal to you in light of that today. Please forgive me for what I've done. I have nowhere to turn except to you, for you alone can cleanse me of the sin that so easily darkens my soul. I turn away from it, and I turn to you, O just One. I don't want to continue in the pattern I've walked for many years, and I am utterly grateful you have stayed with me all my life. I love you. Amen.

DAY THIRTY-THREE

DAVID

Purify me from my sins, and I will be clean; wash me, and I
will be whiter than snow. Oh, give me back my joy again; you
have broken me—now let me rejoice. Don't keep looking at my
sins. Remove the stain of my guilt.

PSALM 51:7-9

This is the continuation of King David's repentance prayer from
yesterday. Note the cleaning terminology here: *purify, clean,
wash, whiter, stain.* Throughout the Old Testament, we see the priests
offering sacrifices for the people. These sacrifices were offered continually, and they could never truly remove the guilt of sin.

Hebrews 10:1 so perfectly captures this predicament: "The old system under the law of Moses was only a shadow, a dim preview of the
good things to come, not the good things themselves. The sacrifices
under that system were repeated again and again, year after year, but
they were never able to provide perfect cleansing for those who came
to worship."

David knew that the only way to truly have a cleared conscience
was to appeal to God directly. He understood that ultimately God is
the One who cleanses the sinner. This psalm echoed and foretold of the
Messiah to come, Jesus Christ, who would, once and for all, offer the
perfect sacrifice. We now live in that age of grace, where we can appeal
to Jesus for continual, sustained cleansing from sin. What a privilege!

Three times in Psalm 51:7-12, David moves away from cleansing
metaphors to joy: "Give me back my joy again"; "Now let me rejoice"

(verse 8); "Restore to me the joy of your salvation" (verse 12). When we are mired in sin, active in hiding our darkness, joy vanishes. But when we confess our sins to the only One who can restore us, joy floods back into our lives. That's the power of grace in the life of the sinner, and it manifests itself in jubilee.

David also asks that God would not take the Holy Spirit from him (verse 11). This is an Old Covenant prayer; during that time, the Holy Spirit alighted on people, but could just as easily leave them. When John the Baptist baptizes Jesus, we see the Holy Spirit similarly alighting on Jesus, but the Scripture tells us the Spirit remained on him (see John 1:32). And now, after Jesus's death and resurrection, the Holy Spirit indwells every new believer. He cannot leave us or forsake us. We will never experience his absence.

> Jesus, you alone can make me clean. Your blood poured out for me on the cross perfectly atones for my sin. There will never be a need for another sacrifice. Thank you for washing me. I long to see my life poured out before you in joy. Beckon me to experience that kind of forgiven joy. And thank you for giving me the Holy Spirit, who is my constant, ever-present companion on this earth. I am grateful. Amen.

DAY THIRTY-FOUR
DAVID

I will teach your ways to rebels, and they will return to you.
Forgive me for shedding blood, O God who saves; then I
will joyfully sing of your forgiveness. Unseal my lips, O Lord,
that my mouth may praise you. You do not desire a sacrifice,
or I would offer one. You do not want a burnt offering. The
sacrifice you desire is a broken spirit. You will not reject
a broken and repentant heart, O God.

PSALM 51:13-17

As King David continues this groundbreaking prayer of repentance, he talks about genuine life change. Once he's experienced the audacious compassion and forgiveness of God, he cannot help but share that journey with others.

It is the same with us. Our testing becomes our testimony. Our mess, I've heard it said, becomes our greatest message. What once derailed us now becomes our determination to live differently.

Throughout this prayer, you see David's heart of repentance. He continues to ask God to forgive the guilt of his sin, particularly the sin of murder. In his brokenness over his sin, he longs to be restored, and he recognizes God as the only restorer.

One of the side effects of long-standing, harbored sin is a leashed tongue. It sticks to the roof of our mouths, unable to praise God. We keep our silence instead of joyfully offering praises to God. David rightly asks God to free his tongue so he can return to the act of worship. He knows that God created us to worship our Creator, and that something painful happens to our souls when we're prevented from praising.

What does God require of us, those who want to praise him? Repentance, yes. But also brokenness. Our inability to carry on, our fears, the worries that keep us up at night—all these are welcome mats for the presence of God. He longs for relationship with us, and that relationship grows in the soil of our sadness and incapability.

So many of us fear approaching God when we have failed. But this prayer reminds us that God delights in coming near to the one who is hurting.

Jesus, I come to you empty-handed, and my heart is hurting. Life has broken me. I have broken myself. I am in pieces, but you alone are the One who can piece me back together. I am grateful I don't have to have my life all together for you to be able to approach me. Renew my joy like the coming of dawn. I surrender again to you. Amen.

DAY THIRTY-FIVE

DAVID

*Please, God, rescue me! Come quickly, LORD, and help
me…I am poor and needy; please hurry to my aid, O God.
You are my helper and my savior; O LORD, do not delay.*

PSALM 70:1,5

Psalm 70 is another psalm of David, a prayer of rescue—one we
can pray daily when life careens around corners, out of control.
This is the prayer we pray when sickness breaks through our mundane
lives, when a loved one faces a crisis, or when death haunts our family.
In the midst of all the heartache that this world offers, we have a rescuing God who loves to answer "Rescue me" prayers.

This prayer is also extremely honest. King David has very real enemies who are bent on ruining him, who applaud his downfalls, who
scheme to harm him (verses 2-3). They take great delight in his failure. Have you ever had a relationship like that? Where you could do
no right, and the other person seemed to be happiest when you were
at your worst?

We can bring our authentic struggles, particularly in difficult relationships, to the throne of God. We can ask God to take notice of
threats or the times when evil seems to triumph over us. We can know
that God is intimately acquainted with our grief.

Yes, just like King David, we are "poor and needy." And so often
that poverty and want come from the relational sins of others against
us. They act as thorns in the flesh, of which the apostle Paul so elo-
quently wrote (see 2 Corinthians 12:7-10).

But just as the thorns informed Paul's weakness, that very weakness became strength when God intervened. In light of that paradox, we can learn to thank God for our difficult relationships, because when they weaken us, we run to our best source of strength.

Jesus, I am hurting. Others have said things over the course of my life that have wounded me. Those words spoken over and over again have weakened me. They have become pesky thorns that have bled my resolve. Instead of letting those words fester and form into feelings of worthlessness, I pray I would turn to you, O God of my strength. Amen.

DAY THIRTY-SIX

ASAPH

*God presides over heaven's court; he pronounces judgment on
the heavenly beings: "How long will you hand down unjust
decisions by favoring the wicked? Give justice to the poor
and the orphan; uphold the rights of the oppressed and the
destitute. Rescue the poor and helpless; deliver them from
the grasp of evil people. But these oppressors know nothing;
they are so ignorant! They wander about in darkness,
while the whole world is shaken to the core."*

PSALM 82:1-5

This is a psalm of Asaph. He was a Levite—one of the three King
David commissioned to conduct singing services in the tabernacle (see 1 Chronicles 16; 25). He was known as a highly adept musician with a prophetic bent. In this psalm we see him declaring God as
the righteous Judge, as the One who presides over the earth in fairness.
In Psalm 82:1, Asaph sees God as the One who can hand out judgment
to angelic beings.

In this prayer, Asaph appeals to God to see the oppression on the
earth and to act in a just manner. He laments the prevalence of wickedness on the earth, which so often means that outcasts, the least, and
the lost are treated with contempt and unfairness.

As if reminding himself (something we need to do as well), he
recounts that those who harm others are unintelligent and ultimately
stagger around in their own darkness. What an apt but sad metaphor
for the wickedness we still see today. One jaunt on the 24-hour news
cycle is enough to convince us of this truth.

Our heart cry can echo Asaph's. We can ask God, our just and righteous Judge, to rouse himself and expose those who continually do harm to the vulnerable (verse 8). We can also, through the power of the Holy Spirit, be the hands and feet of our God in this world. We can be the answer to these imprecatory prayers by exposing evil and darkness and not tolerating criminal activity against the poor and needy.

We are more like God when we take note of those who suffer at the hands of others. Yes, "the whole world is shaken to the core" (verse 5). But God's perfect justice will not be shaken. Every violent, thieving, murderous person will die, and if they die apart from Christ, they will face a just judgment. These are not verses we highlight in Christian art, but they are true, and they bring solace to those who suffer today.

Jesus, take note of this violent world in which I live. Please bring justice, especially for those who suffer. Greed has fueled many sins, causing people to exploit others, and it makes me sad. But I am choosing today to trust that you will make all things right. Amen.

DAY THIRTY-SEVEN
ETHAN THE EZRAHITE

Righteousness and justice are the foundation of your throne.
Unfailing love and truth walk before you as attendants. Happy
are those who hear the joyful call to worship, for they will walk
in the light of your presence, LORD. They rejoice all day long in
your wonderful reputation. They exult in your righteousness.
You are their glorious strength. It pleases you to make us strong.

PSALM 89:14-17

Psalm 89 was penned by Ethan the Ezrahite, a Levite who was known to be almost as wise as King Solomon (see 1 Kings 4:31). Throughout the psalm we catch Ethan singing praises to God. (Yes, singing can be a prayer!)

In this prayer of declaration, we see Ethan's strong theology as he reminisces on the power of God. He sees God as King, sitting on a throne founded on righteousness and justice. As such an immovable trait, it is interesting to see the compassion of God referred to as "love and truth walk[ing] before you as attendants" (Psalm 89:14).

As New Testament Christians, the call to worship God is constant, and we always have the privilege of worshipping our Lord at any time. Because the Spirit of God resides within us, we are constantly reminded of his presence while we walk along the pathways of life, no matter how they twist and turn.

Worship is about who is worthy—the triune God: God the Father, God the Son, and God the Holy Spirit. The Godhead, three in One, is utterly worthy of our affection, praise, and honor. The triune God has an impeccable reputation, and because of that, we bow down in worship. Worship is not about us; it's about ascribing to God all he is worth.

In the act of worship, we experience the paradox of God—that when we are weak, he empowers us. It is his delight to do so. Consider the phraseology in verse 17: "You are their glorious strength. It pleases you to make us strong." Our powerful God is generous with his power. For those who lack vigor, he increases their strength. Not only that, but it also brings him joy when he pours out his vitality upon us.

All we need to do is ask. Like Ethan, we tell God about his amazingness. We choose to worship him because of it. And then we seek his strength and protection. What a blessing to know that God loves to act on our behalf when we approach him!

> Jesus, you are awesome. You are the strength of my life. You are the hope I cling to, the powerful One, the good One. Oh, how I worship you because you are utterly worthy of my songs and prayers. I sing to you, O my strength. I await your protection and affection. Amen.

DAY THIRTY-EIGHT
MOSES

*O LORD, come back to us! How long will you delay? Take pity
on your servants! Satisfy us each morning with your unfailing
love, so we may sing for joy to the end of our lives. Give us
gladness in proportion to our former misery! Replace the evil
years with good. Let us, your servants, see you work again; let
our children see your glory. And may the Lord our God show us
his approval and make our efforts successful.
Yes, make our efforts successful!*

PSALM 90:13-17

This prayer of Moses is frank.

He is flustered and broken by the seeming slowness of God's response to tragedy and pain. He sees misery and complaint. He acknowledges the very real presence of evil. He notes the length of the evil years he and his companions have experienced. So he makes supplication—a request—to God to intervene.

Moses was known to be the man who spoke to God face-to-face (see Exodus 33:11). He had the ear of the Almighty. And yet, even he experienced delays in responses. Even he grew discouraged when evil propagated and proliferated upon the earth.

So he prayed. Honestly. He asked God to pity them all. He reminded God of his unfailing love. And he prayed a prayer of reversal: misery to gladness, good for evil.

We can pray similarly. We can ask God to turn our poverty to provision, fear to faith, worry to worship, pain to praise. He is the God of the great reversal.

Moses ends his prayer by asking for success, for God's people to see the fruit of their labors. Many of us have experienced toil without reward, where we simply work-work-work and do not see fruit. It is good and right to seek God for this kind of success, to see the work of our hands make a difference in the world. Paul reminds us, "Work willingly at whatever you do, as though you were working for the Lord rather than for people. Remember that the Lord will give you an inheritance as your reward, and that the Master you are serving is Christ" (Colossians 3:23-34).

Jesus, I confess that the evil in this world often determines my level of joy or lack thereof. Please have mercy upon those in my life (including me) who struggle. Turn our weariness to dancing. Revamp our joy. Return to us the joy of your salvation, and please let the work of our hands see their reward. I trust you. Amen.

DAY THIRTY-NINE
DAVID

*My heart is confident in you, O God; no wonder I can sing
your praises with all my heart! Wake up, lyre and harp! I will
wake the dawn with my song. I will thank you, LORD, among
all the people. I will sing your praises among the nations. For
your unfailing love is higher than the heavens. Your faithfulness
reaches to the clouds. Be exalted, O God, above the highest
heavens. May your glory shine over all the earth.*

PSALM 108:1-5

King David writes an important truth in this psalm—our need of a confident heart. So many times when we approach God in prayer, we lack confidence. We feel unworthy, incapable of expressing our needs to God, or just too small for him to care about us. Of course, the truth is that God delights in our sacrifices of communication with him. There are no staid rules for approaching him other than simply being ourselves and honestly communicating with him.

We may lack confidence, but God promises he will be our confidence. Proverbs 3:26 reminds us, "The LORD will be your confidence and will keep your foot from being caught" (ESV). On our own, yes, we may stumble, but with the Lord's help empowering us, we can exude confidence in knowing he loves us.

In Hebrews 4:16, we're reminded that we can always approach God's throne, which is no longer a throne of judgment for the believer, but a throne of grace: "Let us come boldly to the throne of our gracious God. There we will receive his mercy, and we will find grace to help us when we need it most."

Because of this confidence and God's extravagant grace, we sing—with everything within us. We awake with a song on our lips. We continue our days with a melody of grace informing our moments. We joyfully sing among others while we extol the virtues of our great God. When life is difficult, when circumstances threaten our resolve, when it is hard to see through thick darkness, praise is our weapon upward. It's our way out of the doldrums, directing our thoughts heavenward. When we praise the goodness of God, we don't have space to dwell on our predicaments.

Whether we praise God or don't does not negate his glory. It still shines powerfully upon this earth. God still sits on the throne. He continues to pursue us and love us, even when our strength ebbs. Even so, take a moment to praise God today. He is worthy.

Jesus, thank you that your love and grace inspire confidence. In myself, I feel small, but in you, I am strengthened and given favor. I am your child—it's almost too much to write. I am so grateful for you. I choose today to praise you for who you are. I love you. I need you. I want to honor you with my day. Amen.

DAY FORTY

Unknown Psalmist

*The LORD has done amazing things for us! What joy! Restore our
fortunes, LORD, as streams renew the desert. Those who plant
in tears will harvest with shouts of joy. They weep as they go to
plant their seed, but they sing as they return with the harvest.*

PSALM 126:3-6

This anonymous psalm is one of the pilgrimage psalms that comprise Psalms 120–134. They're also known as psalms of ascent because they were meant to be sung on the ascent toward Jerusalem, a city situated on a high hill. Anyone traveling to Jerusalem would have to hike. During the festivals and holidays, pilgrims would sing these songs as they approached the holy city. Because of the musicality of these psalms, many verses have made their way into our hymns and choruses.

The theme of Psalm 126 is this: God has done amazing things, so we should praise him. In the first few verses, the psalmist recounts the return of the exiles and the wonder the people experienced when they gratefully returned to their homeland. Surely God had wrought such a miracle, and in light of that, they rejoiced. They went from exiled and homeless to welcomed and provided for.

This idea is echoed in our salvation. Once, we were far from God, exiled by sin—but through Jesus Christ, we have been brought near. The apostle Paul reminds us in Ephesians 2:13: "Once you were far away from God, but now you have been brought near to him through the blood of Christ."

But even after we find Jesus, we still struggle and suffer. We still cry out. We weep as we plant seeds. But this psalm of ascent reminds us that our toil is not in vain. We may cry, but one day we will reap a harvest. We may wait upon fallow ground, but God will bring fruit. We may walk dejected and thirsty in the desert, but God promises to be a stream of living water to our parched soul.

The God of the reversal sees you. He takes note of your work, every tear and worry. He will never leave you. He will not abandon you. Today you have the opportunity to believe that, to say these truths to him in joy and gratitude.

Jesus, I can ascend to your holy hill because you ascended the hill of Calvary, once and for all. My soul-fortunes can be reversed because of your life, death, and resurrection. I choose to praise you in the desert. I choose to praise you as I plant my seeds with tears. I choose to believe you will reward my hard work. I love you. Amen.

DAY FORTY-ONE

ISAIAH

*It's all over! I am doomed, for I am a sinful man. I have filthy
lips, and I live among a people with filthy lips. Yet I have
seen the King, the LORD of Heaven's Armies.*

ISAIAH 6:5

The prophet Isaiah wrote this after an encounter with God, seeing him on a grand throne while his robe filled the heavenly temple. Six-winged seraphim attended God. Two wings covered their eyes, two covered their feet, and the third set of wings kept them in flight. They proclaimed, "Holy, holy, holy is the LORD of Heaven's Armies! The whole earth is filled with his glory!" (Isaiah 6:3). Prior to Isaiah's woe-is-me declaration, the voices of the seraphim made the temple's foundations quake, while smoke filled the area.

Can you imagine witnessing such majesty and grandeur?

When confronted by the otherness of God, his utmost holiness, repentance is the only right response. Isaiah's first words after this encounter were confessional: He was sinful. He spoke sinful words. He lived among sinners. One hundred percent of us could say the same thing. We are sinners (thankfully saved by grace). We utter awful words. We live among sinners who are bent toward wrongdoing.

Confession is a form of prayer—a powerful one. Have you ever been in a relationship in which someone has truly wronged you but will not admit their failure? How does that relationship play itself out? Because of the offense, what was once a viable, affable friendship morphs into distance. But when that person humbly and specifically apologizes, relationship has the opportunity to reflourish.

It is the same with God. When we fail to confess our sins (since all our sins are ultimately against him), we distance ourselves from our relational God. Only when we fess up to our waywardness can relationship resume.

> Jesus, I am sorry. I confess this specific sin to you. You have convicted me of it, and I no longer want to carry it. Please forgive me. Please restore our relationship according to your goodness. You are holy. I am not. But I am utterly grateful for your Holy Spirit within me, who empowers me today to embrace the holiness you offer. Amen.

DAY FORTY-TWO

JEREMIAH

LORD, you always give me justice when I bring a case before you. So let me bring you this complaint: Why are the wicked so prosperous? Why are evil people so happy? You have planted them, and they have taken root and prospered. Your name is on their lips, but you are far from their hearts.

JEREMIAH 12:1-2

"Why are the wicked so prosperous?" It's a question every human being has asked of the world, and especially of God. It seems he is silent. It seems he is absent. It seems he doesn't engage in the matter of evil.

It's important to note that Jeremiah—or any prophet, for that matter—is not sanctioned for asking such a bold question. This honesty is prayer. God is not interested in our platitudes or us playing nice when we're curious or frustrated or enraged. He wants honesty. He welcomes questions. Why? Because his primary interest is having a strong relationship with his children, and questions foster that.

In this prayer, Jeremiah, the "weeping prophet," reminds God of his justice before he renders his complaint. He sincerely wants to know why wicked people seem so carefree and happy. He recognizes God created these people, and he also uncovers their hypocrisy. His words echo the Lord's in the book of Isaiah: "They honor me with their lips, but their hearts are far from me" (29:13). (Note that Jesus quotes this in Matthew 15:8.)

This reveals that Jeremiah's complaint is not against random wicked people, but those who act wickedly while the name of God is on their tongue. Taking this reality forward to modern day, it is right to be befuddled and angry about people who attend church but harm others. It is right to voice this concern to God. It is right to ask that God would uncover what is hidden, that he would expose hypocrisy. Judgment, it is said, will begin in the house of God (see 1 Peter 4:17).

As we pray that liars would be exposed, predators would be found out, and religious oppressors revealed, it's also important that we ask God to search our hearts as well. We are not immune to harming others by saying one thing but doing another—all while claiming the name of Christ.

Jesus, help me navigate a world where people in church—often leaders!—harm others. Bring justice. Shed your holy light on those who oppress others. Help me realize your justice holds hands with your love. And as I pray this, please search my heart. I don't want to live a life of hypocrisy. Amen.

DAY FORTY-THREE

JEREMIAH

*LORD, see my anguish! My heart is broken and my soul despairs,
for I have rebelled against you. In the streets the sword kills, and
at home there is only death. Others heard my groans, but no
one turned to comfort me. When my enemies heard about my
troubles, they were happy to see what you had done. Oh, bring
the day you promised, when they will suffer as I have suffered.*

LAMENTATIONS 1:20-21

Jeremiah's prayer here is utterly frank. He does not shy away from detailing his anguish. He uses words like *broken, despairs, groans, troubles,* and *suffer.* Not only that, but his is an imprecatory prayer. He asks God to take notice of his enemies and pay them back for the wrong they have inflicted.

This is not a popular theology, as we constantly hear the refrain of affectionate love in our worship songs. God loves us, yes. God's love extends to all, yes. But his love is one aspect of his character. He is also holy, holy, holy—this triple emphasis being the only of its kind in Scripture. (God is not referred to as "loving, loving, loving," for example.) It is permissible to call on the rightness of God, to ask him to make things right.

In light of that, we must also remember Romans 12:19, which tells us, "Dear friends, never take revenge. Leave that to the righteous anger of God. For the Scriptures say, 'I will take revenge; I will pay them back,' says the LORD." Our perfect and just God knows all things. He searches all hearts. He knows motivations—something impossible for us to discern even in ourselves. If we strive to enact vengeance, it will be incomplete, without all the facts.

God is perfectly capable of seeing all humankind beneath his gaze. He is best equipped to provide justice—if not in this life, then in the next.

There is great comfort in knowing that all we have suffered has meaning, and that unrepentant people who have harmed many will face their actions.

Jesus, thank you that I can be honest in my prayers. I can share my defeats and worries with you, and you welcome my ruminations about trauma and fear. Thank you that you also care about justice, and that your vengeance will be perfectly meted out. I take my hands off revenge, and, instead, entrust my way and heart to you. Amen.

DAY FORTY-FOUR

JEREMIAH

O LORD, think about this! Should you treat your own
people this way? Should mothers eat their own children,
those they once bounced on their knees? Should priests and
prophets be killed within the Lord's Temple? See them lying
in the streets—young and old, boys and girls, killed by the
swords of the enemy. You have killed them in your anger,
slaughtering them without mercy.

LAMENTATIONS 2:20-21

Jeremiah prayed these painfully honest words during one of the darkest times in the history of Israel, when their enemies forcibly took them into exile. In that unprecedented calamity, the prophet's words weep.

Jeremiah is in the middle of his narrative, where he knows the beginning but cannot see his way to the end. Every good novel has this dark moment, where it seems nothing good can happen and only evil will prevail.

Have you ever felt that way? Are you in the middle of your story, where you cannot see a bend in the road or a light emanating from the future? Jeremiah offers an honest framework of prayer here for us. He begs God to look upon them, to see what is happening, and to provide relief from their very real agony. He intercedes for the suffering of others—something countless Bible study groups do for their members and those with whom the members have relationships, as everyone lists their prayer concerns.

Are you heavyhearted today? Pray. Are there burdens you cannot drop? Pray. Do you have friends or family members who seem Job-like, constantly battling pain or oppression or fear? Pray. Are you confused by God's seeming indifference? Pray. Are you weary from a battle that appears to have no end? Pray. Are you losing your grip on hope? Pray.

Jeremiah's example grants permission for every pilgrim on this earth to lament. To weep. To be authentic. To give God the gift of vulnerability. In that circle of honesty, you can find solace, knowing God hears every lament, every question, every agony.

> Jesus, thank you that I can come to you with questions. Thank you that I don't have to understand evil or realize why evil happens to lament about it to you. I lift up that person in my life who is suffering. Would you take notice, Lord? Would you relieve pain? Would you help me know how to pray more specifically and ardently? Amen.

DAY FORTY-FIVE

JEREMIAH

*Joy has left our hearts; our dancing has turned to
mourning. The garlands have fallen from our heads. Weep
for us because we have sinned. Our hearts are sick and
weary, and our eyes grow dim with tears. For Jerusalem is
empty and desolate, a place haunted by jackals.*

LAMENTATIONS 5:15-18

Again we see the weeping prophet Jeremiah pouring out everything before the God he loves. He echoes what many people
experience today—a deep depression, a despondency that comes from
extremely difficult and traumatic circumstances. It's as if he is writing in
our contemporary world. Sin and its consequences have not changed.

There are places on this earth where evil prevails, where human
beings are trafficked, where wars prompt rape, where the rich gleefully
oppress the poor while living lavishly, where politicians spin lies like
cotton candy. Jeremiah rightly laments this. He rightly calls Jerusalem
"a place haunted by jackals," an empty, desolate wasteland.

There is loneliness hanging in his words. When evil preys upon a
people and nation, isolation results. That feeling that no one else can
understand the heart's bitterness morphs into a profound angst.

But there is hope. God does see. He does take note of our sorrows.
Psalm 56:8-11 reminds us,

> You keep track of all my sorrows. You have collected all my
> tears in your bottle. You have recorded each one in your
> book. My enemies will retreat when I call to you for help.

This I know: God is on my side! I praise God for what he has promised; yes, I praise the LORD for what he has promised. I trust in God, so why should I be afraid? What can mere mortals do to me?

Today may be steeped in darkness, but our God, who is marvelous light, will bring hope again. Our only job is to stay connected to him, and we do that by honestly sharing our woes with our Wonderful Counselor, who takes note of our sorrow.

Someday all this pain will make sense. It's okay if it doesn't today. Our sovereign God has a mysterious plan that will unfold in splendor. But in the in-between time, when life plummets toward sadness, rest in knowing he sees you.

Jesus, I am hurting. I don't even know how to talk about my grief. But I choose to let you know my anger and bewilderment anyway. Thank you for taking note of my tears. Thank you that even though today makes no sense, I can rest in your plan. I trust you, or at least I try to. Amen.

DAY FORTY-SIX

EZEKIEL

O Sovereign LORD, must I be defiled by using human dung?
For I have never been defiled before. From the time I was a
child until now I have never eaten any animal that died of
sickness or was killed by other animals. I have never eaten
any meat forbidden by the law.

EZEKIEL 4:14

The unusual circumstances surrounding this odd-sounding prayer must be highlighted in order to understand the prophet Ezekiel's lament. At the beginning of Ezekiel 4, God instructs him to build a model of Jerusalem, complete with siege ramps. Then he is to lie on his left side, bearing the weight of Israel's sins for three hundred ninety days, "one day for each year of their sin" (verse 5). After that he is to lie on his right side for forty days, one day for every year of Judah's sin. All while prophesying. After giving these instructions, God tells him to bake bread from various grains during the days he is lying on his left side, using human dung as the fire's fuel.

It's interesting that Ezekiel's protest isn't against building a model, lying on one side and then the next, or the duration of his reclining, but against the particular fuel for the fire. In Deuteronomy 23:12-14, God instructs the nation of Israel on what to do with their human excrement—it is to be buried outside the camp, where everything that is defiled lives. So to use human dung would be a defiling act.

Logically, it makes sense that, in the depiction of a siege where the nation of Israel is killing all their animals for food, one would find animal dung scarce. Yet Ezekiel balks, and God relents. "All right," the

Lord says. "You may bake your bread with cow dung instead of human dung" (Ezekiel 4:15).

This exchange reveals something strangely beautiful about God's nature: He is moved by our honest worry. He is concerned with our concern. He has mercy upon his children who cry out to him.

You may find yourself in a worrisome situation. You may be living on the brink of desperation in a conundrum that is not your fault (Ezekiel suffered on behalf of a sinning people). But God does see. He listens to your cries for help. He takes note of your suffering. He understands when you are wrongly accused or bearing the consequences of someone else's actions. He is the God of the seemingly impossible situation—a place where Ezekiel lived.

Jesus, I come to you with desperate pleading, much like Ezekiel did here. Would you find a pathway for me to walk that is not defiling? Would you deliver me from this predicament? Would you renew my hope like the dawn's rising? I am in need. I am worried. Help me. Amen.

DAY FORTY-SEVEN

EZEKIEL

*While they were out killing, I was all alone. I fell face down on
the ground and cried out, "O Sovereign LORD! Will your fury
against Jerusalem wipe out everyone left in Israel?"... While I was
still prophesying, Pelatiah son of Benaiah suddenly died. Then I
fell face down on the ground and cried out, "O Sovereign LORD,
are you going to kill everyone in Israel?"*

EZEKIEL 9:8; 11:13

Desperation fuels these anguished prayers. At this time, God is
allowing an external nation to pillage the nation of Israel in
siege. This is his judgment upon the people who continually disobeyed
his commandments, particularly by revering and worshipping other
gods, practicing licentious idolatry. God sent prophets warning Israel
of what would happen, but the nation, stiff-necked, refused to listen.

And now Ezekiel lives in the midst of this egregious siege, feeling utterly alone, anguished beyond words. The sky is falling in his
vision and in his nation, and it seems like he alone is left to bear the
aftereffects.

Have you ever felt completely alone in your suffering? Have you
fallen to your face in grief? Have tears become as common as your
daily coffee?

In the midst of such terrible, unprecedented turmoil, what does
Ezekiel do? He prays. He cries out to God, the only One who can rescue him. His dogged desperation keeps him pinned to God, and he
makes a conscious choice not to abandon the Almighty God.

You hear echoes of this kind of determination in John 6. Jesus had preached a very difficult teaching about eating his flesh and drinking his blood. It was so offensive that many of his disciples abandoned him. He asked the Twelve, "Are you also going to leave?" (verse 67).

Peter said these words: "Lord, to whom would we go? You have the words that give eternal life" (verse 68).

When life is bleak and answers are few, we do have a choice. We can abandon the God who doesn't make sense in that moment, or we can do as the disciples did and as Ezekiel exemplified—we can pray to our loving God, seeking "the words that give eternal life."

Jesus, I don't pretend to understand everything that flurries around me. I confess there are times I give in to desperation. Life sometimes puts me on my face. Even though I don't comprehend the whys, I choose to turn to you, the sovereign One. Where else could I go? Amen.

DAY FORTY-EIGHT

DANIEL

*I prayed to the LORD my God and confessed: "O Lord,
you are a great and awesome God! You always fulfill
your covenant and keep your promises of unfailing love
to those who love you and obey your commands. But we
have sinned and done wrong. We have rebelled against
you and scorned your commands and regulations. We
have refused to listen to your servants the prophets, who
spoke on your authority to our kings and princes and
ancestors and to all the people of the land."*

DANIEL 9:4-6

Daniel lived in exile, yet he continued his life of prayer. He begins
this lengthy prayer that lasts 16 verses with praise of the character of his God. He calls God "great" (greater than him, greater than
circumstances, greater than nature) and "awesome" (utterly different
from humankind—powerful, inspiring, intelligent).

He reminds God of his fidelity—as the One who keeps his promises as a covenantal Creator.

And then this conjunction interrupts his revelry: *but*. "But we have
sinned and done wrong" (Daniel 9:5). In this petition, Daniel does not
confess his personal sins. Instead, he admits to the sins of his nation.
He demonstrates what substitutionary repentance looks like. Though
he bears no guilt for his nation's sins, he confesses them on behalf of
that unrepentant people—those to whom God had sent continuous
warning.

Daniel uses words like *rebelled, scorned, refused*—strong words that do not reflect Daniel's character, but indict Israel's. Those stiff-necked sins are what caused Daniel's predicament of living in exile.

Daniel does not use pronouns like *them* or *they*. No, he owns those sins as if they were his own. He uses *we*. "*We* have sinned" (verse 5, emphasis added).

This "we" prayer points forward to the day when Jesus would bear the weight of sins he did not commit on the cross. He would take the fall for atrocities and offenses he did not enact. He, the innocent One, would identify with a sinful people in order to save them.

We have the privilege to pray as Daniel did. We, too, can confess the sins of our towns, cities, states, and nations. We can repent on behalf of evil in our midst. As we do this, we reflect the heartbeat of Jesus, who interceded for those who were guilty.

Jesus, I live in a sin-infused nation, among stubborn people who rebel against your commands. I confess the sins of murder, greed, idolatry, gossip, theft, and so much more. Please have mercy upon my nation. I pray for revival. I pray for your presence here. I pray for hope in the midst of a crooked and perverse generation. Amen.

DAY FORTY-NINE

DANIEL

I heard what he said, but I did not understand what he meant.
So I asked, "How will all this finally end, my lord?"

DANIEL 12:8

Daniel has a vision in which he sees a man who is dressed in linen, and eventually two others. One of those "others" asks the man in linen how long all the "shocking events" Daniel has just learned about will endure (Daniel 12:6). The man in linen vaguely answers, "It will go on for a time, times, and half a time" (verse 7). This is when Daniel asks the clarifying question we see in today's devotion.

The man in linen, who some believe to be a theophany (an appearance of Jesus Christ before he later incarnated), answers, "Go now, Daniel, for what I have said is kept secret and sealed until the time of the end" (verse 9). This is curiously similar to Jesus's response in Acts 1 when the disciples ask if Jesus will now restore the kingdom to Israel. He says, "The Father alone has the authority to set those dates and times, and they are not for you to know" (verse 7).

We now live in the era of grace, where Jesus sits at the right hand of the throne of God, interceding for us. Like in this exchange with Daniel and the conversation with his disciples, Jesus will also welcome our questions, but he may not always answer them. Some things are to remain a mystery. Our curiosity will not always be satisfied.

We live in the tension of the now and the not yet. This is why we must exercise faith, acting on it even if we don't understand what is happening around us. That's why it's called "faith"—trusting in what we do not yet see, moving forward though life may be perplexing.

There is solace, though, in knowing we do not have to know all the answers. We don't have to know the specifics of the end of the story to be able to live well. We choose to trust the words of our Lord in that tension of unknowing.

It is normal to ask questions, but it is also normal not to receive every answer. Sometimes we are called to trust, to wait on God to unfold the perfectly executed plan he is enacting. We may not know the eras of time, but we know the One who holds them all in the palm of his hand. We may not know the outcome of our painful situation, but we do know that God sees our stories from beginning to end, and that he is a good Father who leads his children well.

Jesus, thank you that you do not balk when I ask you a question. I trust you to answer when it's necessary for my growth and refrain when the information is not mine to know. I am not God. You are. I choose to follow you in the mystery, in the place between now and not yet. Amen.

DAY FIFTY

AMOS

*In my vision the locusts ate every green plant in sight. Then
I said, "O Sovereign LORD, please forgive us or we will not
survive, for Israel is so small." So the LORD relented from this
plan. "I will not do it," he said. Then the Sovereign LORD
showed me another vision. I saw him preparing to punish his
people with a great fire. The fire had burned up the depths of
the sea and was devouring the entire land. Then I said, "O
Sovereign LORD, please stop or we will not survive, for Israel is
so small." Then the LORD relented from this plan, too.*

AMOS 7:2-6

There is power in prayer. And in relationship. In this portion of
Amos, we see the minor prophet interceding on behalf of his
nation after some very disturbing visions of locusts and fire. God, after
hearing Amos's pleas, relents. This means he chooses not to destroy
Israel with bugs or burns.

This invites some pesky questions. Does God change his mind?
Do we follow a capricious God who chooses one avenue, then flips
the script? Are we that powerful, able to change the mind and direction of God?

It's important to understand that God has unconditional and conditional pronouncements. In unconditional decrees, God makes an
oath he will not change. We see this in 1 Samuel 15:27-29, when he
speaks through Samuel of Saul's absolute demise as king. There is no
condition that will change his mind. The decree is final.

In conditional decrees, God may relent or change his mind

depending on the reaction or repentance of someone. We see this in Exodus 32:12-14, when Moses intercedes on behalf of the children of Israel, and God chooses not to erase them from the earth. Here in Amos, we see the same dynamic, that of a prophet interceding on behalf of a people. [3]

Our sovereign God is mysterious, not easily understood. But this passage should bring hope to the one who loves to pray, especially when praying for those who are far from God. God hears the prayers of the intercessor. He bends his ear to the cries of those who long to see disaster averted from people who make terrible choices. He is both just and merciful, and as we come to him, we absolutely can appeal to his mercy.

Jesus, I pray boldly for my loved ones who are far from you, and I pray for mercy on their behalf. I pray you would help them reach the bottom of themselves so they will stretch their hands and hearts toward you. Please do not allow them to destroy themselves. Have mercy. I pray my loved ones will repent and find you today. Amen.

DAY FIFTY-ONE

SAILORS

*They cried out to the LORD, Jonah's God. "O LORD," they
pleaded, "don't make us die for this man's sin. And don't hold us
responsible for his death. O LORD, you have sent this storm upon
him for your own good reasons."*

JONAH 1:14

When people who don't know God are desperate and facing certain doom, they pray "foxhole prayers" like this. We may consider such prayers in the midst of mayhem ineffective, but God hears the desperate cries of those who face death. He answered this prayer, revealing the seas roiled just for Jonah.

It's ironic that the sailors aboard the ship showed more fear of God than Jonah did, who slept as the ship tossed. And when they fearfully tossed Jonah from the ship, they experienced salvation from the choppy waters.

We can pray for those who are far from the Lord. As they face impossible situations, we can intercede, asking God to prompt them to pray for rescue. For the family member facing suicidal thoughts, we can ask that their mind turn to ultimate questions about life after death and very real fear and trepidation. In those places of abject terror, God loves to step in and rescue.

The sailors who believed in a pantheon of gods spent ample time beseeching their incapable deities to no avail. No matter what kind of perfect verbal wrangling they performed or desperate pleading they yelled, no answer came. When they deduced it was the God Jonah served who authored the storm, they dropped all that feverish god pitching to appeal to the One who created it all.

Sometimes people have to exhaust themselves in chasing other gods before they will turn to the God of the Bible. As an intercessor, you have the unique privilege of praying them through that journey from fruitless searching to fruitful *aha*.

Don't let discouragement strangle your prayers for your loved ones who are far from God. See this as their journey toward deeper levels of unfulfillment. Pray that their eyes will be opened to the shallowness of their pursuit. Pray that they would long for the One who made them. Don't give up. Keep interceding. Perhaps, like the desperate sailors, they will reach heavenward in the storm.

Jesus, I pray for those people in my life who are chasing everything but you. Would you bring them to the end of themselves and that journey? Would you show them that their pleadings to little gods will profit nothing? You are their Creator, their Savior, their loving friend. Please rescue them today. Amen.

DAY FIFTY-TWO

JONAH

*As my life was slipping away, I remembered the LORD. And my
earnest prayer went out to you in your holy Temple. Those who
worship false gods turn their backs on all God's mercies. But I
will offer sacrifices to you with songs of praise, and I will fulfill
all my vows. For my salvation comes from the LORD alone.*

JONAH 2:7-9

One of the most important times for people to pray is when they
face death. Suddenly, everything becomes clear. Life's irregular
focus snaps to clarity. Death strips people of facades, that which they
cling to, and brings them to the edge of their false beliefs.

Here Jonah remembers the rule of God. He remembers his kingdom, kingship, and reign from his holy temple. He understands afresh
that those who chase after fame, possessions, wealth, and personal grandeur will find themselves excessively empty. When people pursue that
which does not ultimately satisfy, they turn their backs on the readily available mercy of God—a mercy he pours out upon his children.

The message here is twofold: We can pray for those who have chased
other gods, asking God to have mercy upon our wayward loved ones.
But we can also be like Jonah—coming back to our senses and returning to God. Both are important prayers—the first intercession, the second confession.

In confession, Jonah renews his commitment to God. He remembers his rebellion and decides to return to sacrificing for God—not
necessarily through animals offered upon an altar, but in his person. He
offers up songs of praise, unfettered worship in gratitude to God for his

very real salvation. Our worship, like Jonah's, is a form of prayer. As we sing, we acknowledge, from deep within our souls, that God deserves our adulation.

Not only does Jonah return spiritually and offer praise, but he also physically repents. He says he will fulfill the vows he made. Through the narrative we find out that Jonah returns to the mission God gave him in the first place—to share the words of God with the Ninevites, who are far from him.

Later in the story, we see the pouting prophet, angry at God's evident mercy. He obeyed God by preaching doom, and when repentance resulted, Jonah could not see the pattern. God had rescued him from himself when he repented. And now God had rescued the people of Nineveh, who did the same. God had mercy upon both Jew and pagan alike—something in which Jonah's prejudice could not rejoice.

Jesus, I pray for those in my life who need rescue by you. I pray they would, like the Ninevites, repent and find you. And, Lord Jesus, would you search my heart too? I do not want to be far from you. Instead of grumbling, I choose to rejoice. Show me my next step, so I can walk toward you in obedience. Amen.

DAY FIFTY-THREE

HABAKKUK

How long, O LORD, must I call for help? But you do not listen! "Violence is everywhere!" I cry, but you do not come to save. Must I forever see these evil deeds? Why must I watch all this misery? Wherever I look, I see destruction and violence. I am surrounded by people who love to argue and fight. The law has become paralyzed, and there is no justice in the courts. The wicked far outnumber the righteous, so that justice has become perverted.

HABAKKUK 1:2-4

The prophet Habakkuk lives in a lawless time, where justice is elusive, people get away with violence, and fighting is predominant. Sounds a lot like the world we live in, doesn't it? Sin has not changed over the past few thousand years. Evil has not lost its pervasiveness.

What are we to do as we pray?

We do as Habakkuk does—we ask questions. We ask, "How long?" We lament. We tell God our predicaments, both personally and corporately. We cry. We detail the misery. We tell the truth. We discern. We observe. We get on our knees and fight the only way we can—with weapons suited for heavenly battles.

Seeing injustice and pointing it out is only half the battle. Acknowledging evil and then exposing it is important, but we must fight this kind of evil with a different kind of ammunition. In Ephesians 6:14-18, the apostle Paul illuminates our warfare:

> Stand your ground, putting on the belt of truth and the body armor of God's righteousness. For shoes, put on the

119

peace that comes from the Good News so that you will be
fully prepared. In addition to all of these, hold up the shield
of faith to stop the fiery arrows of the devil. Put on salvation as your helmet, and take the sword of the Spirit, which
is the word of God. Pray in the Spirit at all times and on
every occasion. Stay alert and be persistent in your prayers
for all believers everywhere.

We wear gospel shoes, the very essence of good news that counter-
attacks the bad news of perversion. Our faith shield protects us from
the assailments of the evil one as he roams the earth, creating havoc.
Our salvation helmet keeps the lies from rooting into our thoughts.
The very word of God is our offensive weapon we use in prayer to dis-
mantle the injustice of this world.

In light of this, remember that to pray the word of God is to render
the enemy of our souls powerless. He cannot stand against it.

Jesus, this is a sin-darkened world full of violence, perversion, and
injustice. But I choose to fight this overwhelming battle with the only
weapon I know—you. Teach me to love your gospel, experience
your peace, and pray your Scripture for every impossible situation
the world throws my way. Amen.

DAY FIFTY-FOUR

HABAKKUK

*Even though the fig trees have no blossoms, and there are no
grapes on the vines; even though the olive crop fails, and the
fields lie empty and barren; even though the flocks die in
the fields, and the cattle barns are empty, yet I will rejoice
in the LORD! I will be joyful in the God of my salvation!
The Sovereign LORD is my strength! He makes me as
surefooted as a deer, able to tread upon the heights.*

HABAKKUK 3:17-19

Before offering this well-known part of his prayer, the prophet
Habakkuk recounts the history of Israel prior to exile. He takes
note of seas being parted, enemies routed, victories won. *All this he
prays while singing.* In his prayer-song he refers to God and his works
as amazing, merciful, holy, splendorous, brilliant, powerful, shatter-
ing, leveling, trampling, rescuing, crushing, and akin to a whirlwind.

Perhaps we should sing our prayers as well. Perhaps we should
trace the deliverance God has wrought on our behalf before we make
requests. Perhaps we should chronicle the beautiful and sometimes terrifying character traits of God before we petition him for help.

All that serves as background for this faith-infused prayer. Habakkuk realizes that circumstances may not return to normal. His expectations may shatter. There may be little hope on to which he can hold.
Yet, because of God's past faithfulness and his current character, there
is cause for joy.

We are not promised perfect provision in this life. There are Christ-
following people around the world who suffer hunger today. There are

many who name Jesus as Lord who are financially broken. Some who follow him in difficult areas will lose their lives for their faith. These are current realities. But there is so much more than the here and now. God's kingdom expands beyond this earth, and one day we will all be filled, provided for, and rescued—in the next life.

Habakkuk has this type of heavenly mind-set, an eternal perspective that dares to ask for joy in the midst of difficulties. He recognizes that trials meant to test us can also remind us that our own strength is faltering, and we desperately need the strength of God to move forward.

Are you in that place of suffering? Trace the topography of God's faithfulness. Focus on his virtues. Realize that this life is not all there is. And choose to rejoice nonetheless. In that place of weakness, you'll realize the power of God in a unique way.

Jesus, I look back on my life and see your handiwork. I am stunned at how beautifully you have led and protected me. You are powerful, amazing, surprising, and full of compassion. I face an uncertain future. I do not know what will happen next. But I choose to follow you with joy as my companion. Amen.

DAY FIFTY-FIVE

JESUS

*Pray like this: Our Father in heaven, may your name be
kept holy. May your Kingdom come soon. May your will
be done on earth, as it is in heaven. Give us today the food
we need, and forgive us our sins, as we have forgiven those
who sin against us. And don't let us yield to temptation,
but rescue us from the evil one.*

MATTHEW 6:9-13

The epitome of prayer is encapsulated in the Lord's Prayer. Jesus
teaches his disciples the essential nature of prayer in such few
words, ones worth unpacking.

First, we begin everything by prayer. When life tumbles out of
control, we pray. When we are sick, we pray. When circumstances go
south, we pray. When life is good, we pray.

When we pray, we remember the corporate nature of prayer. This
prayer does not begin, "My Father in heaven." Powerful prayer occurs
alongside other believers.

The holiness of God must infuse our petitions. In recognizing his
holiness, we state that without him, we are not. There is a repentant
bent to this prayer.

As we pray, we long to see the kingdom of God emerge in our context—that great upside-down kingdom where the small are strengthened, the overlooked are dignified, and the hurting are validated. We
can ask that we would be positive agents in this surprising kingdom.

Of course, our prayer must also be infused with a desire to see God's
will accomplished on this earth—that people would be set free from

their sins and vices and addictions, that evil would be illuminated and vanquished, that salvation would be preached by no other name.

After all this worship and kingdom language, we ask God for our needs—for food, life, breath, health.

We confess our sins, asking Jesus for the forgiveness he so beautifully bestows. And in light of that forgiveness, we choose to radically extend grace to others.

Finally, we end our prayer by tackling the problem of evil. We ask for protection from temptation and victory over the darkness.

Jesus, thank you for this model prayer. You are so good. You are so strong. You are worthy of my praise. You are holy. Please help me be a part of building your counterintuitive kingdom. Grant me my needs today. Forgive my sins and give me the wherewithal to forgive those people who have hurt me. Slay evil, Jesus. Amen.

DAY FIFTY-SIX

LEPER

Suddenly, a man with leprosy approached him and knelt
before him. "Lord," the man said, "if you are willing,
you can heal me and make me clean." Jesus reached out
and touched him. "I am willing," he said. "Be healed!"
And instantly the leprosy disappeared.

MATTHEW 8:2-3

When we approach God, it is wise to take the posture of this man with leprosy—that of bold humbleness.

The man epitomized boldness. An outcast from the commonwealth of Israel because of his contagious skin condition, he was certainly not to approach others. He bore his reproach outside the camp (Leviticus 13:45-46)—interestingly, the same place Jesus suffered crucifixion (see Hebrews 13:12-13)—and would have to bear that life alone unless he experienced healing.

Instead of letting that prevent him from approaching Jesus, the known reputation of Jesus compelled him to make his daring request. This points both to this man's faith and the irresistibility of Jesus.

But this man also approached the King of kings and the Lord of lords with humility. He knelt. He knew he stood in the presence of royalty. He didn't presume he'd be welcomed. He submitted. He genuflected. He sat in the place of the learner—humbly at the Rabbi's feet.

We, too, must consider this posture as we approach our holy God in prayer. Because of what Jesus has done on the cross and because of his victory over death in the resurrection, we have unfettered access to him. We can boldly approach him because of his outlandish grace.

But we must recognize our place in that prayer. He is God. We are his children. He is the resurrection and life; we are not. He is the One who spun the universe into glorious existence; we are merely his creation. May it be that we approach our approachable God with reverence.

Jesus, I humble myself before you—even before I ask you for help. Thank you that you have made a way for me to communicate and commune with you because of your life, death, and resurrection. I'm so grateful. Hear my cry today. I feel small, living outside the gate of this world, longing to be noticed. Amen.

DAY FIFTY-SEVEN

ROMAN OFFICER

"Lord, my young servant lies in bed, paralyzed and in terrible pain." Jesus said, "I will come and heal him." But the officer said, "Lord, I am not worthy to have you come into my home. Just say the word from where you are, and my servant will be healed."... Then Jesus said to the Roman officer, "Go back home. Because you believed, it has happened." And the young servant was healed that same hour.

MATTHEW 8:6-8,13

There are three things to keep in mind when considering this story of prayer.

First, it's important to note that the person making this audacious request is not an Israelite. He is a centurion, a Roman officer. This is an unprecedented interaction, someone of high rank within the Roman army subjugating himself before Jesus.

Second, this officer has an intercessory heart for his servant—a rare occurrence in his culture.

Third, he submitted himself to Jesus—who represented a captive nation.

Consider this: The centurion, rich in power and wealth, intrinsically understood that an itinerant preacher with no place to call home had something he did not. Ultimately, Jesus had authority—over sickness, the demonic, the cosmos. Though the officer possessed a semblance of control over his world, he realized that only Jesus commanded the seas and wind.

This man's faith amazed Jesus (Matthew 8:10). Stunned him. And the officer was not from the nation of Israel. This would begin the ongoing journey of reaching Jerusalem, Judea, Samaria, and then the ends of the earth with the gospel (see Acts 1:8). This centurion represented the glorious future of the church—a multiethnic, rich and poor, slave and free, male and female organism that would ultimately permeate the known world.

This story also illustrates the power of the word Jesus utters. He did not directly lay his hands upon the centurion's servant. He simply said the word—something the centurion believed Jesus could do. In the very moment of Jesus's uttering, the hurting servant was healed.

As we approach Jesus, let's keep this in mind. First, if we are not of Jewish roots, we can thank him for including us in the body of Christ. Second, we can follow the example of humility this Roman officer demonstrated. Though he was rich and powerful, he knew the source of true power. And we can trust that the word Jesus utters on our behalf is effective. Let's choose to exercise this kind of faith when we pray.

Jesus, thank you for this example of humility and faith. I want to learn to approach you in this way, to humble myself before you, to recognize my powerlessness, and to ask you for help. I cannot live my life in my own strength and power. No, I need you. I need your strength. I need your intercession and rescue. Amen.

DAY FIFTY-EIGHT

DISCIPLES

The disciples went and woke him up, shouting, "Lord, save us!
We're going to drown!" Jesus responded, "Why are you afraid?
You have so little faith!" Then he got up and rebuked the wind
and waves, and suddenly there was a great calm.

MATTHEW 8:25-26

What must it have been like to experience this scene? So often we read the Bible as if it were an ancient book of stories with little or no relevance for us. We forget that these miracles happened to real people, gritted by daily work, exhausted, and quite human.

One way to experience the narratives of the Gospels is to place yourself firmly in the middle of the story. Feel the wind on your skin. Remember a time when you felt terror in your gut, afraid your current situation would be the end of you. In this passage, the disciples are facing a watery death. They could see no way forward or backward—only spiraling downward into the depths of the sea.

This was not a casual fear.

The disciples shouted. They panicked. They could feel the specter of death in the wind.

Have you ever been in that place? Are you there today? Jesus is waiting for your wake-up call. He will intercede. He will calm the storms and waves of your life. But first you must come to that true place of desperation.

Prayer often sounds like a cry. It resembles a shout of panic. It can be as pedestrian as "Help! I'm drowning here!"

Imagine what it must have been like to cling to the sides of a boat about to sink, without a life jacket or the ability to swim, while thunder and lightning make the sea a torrent, boiling the water into a human-consuming stew. Then imagine Jesus stepping into the chaos, whispering "Silence! Be still!" (Mark 4:39), and all the sea's wrath calming in an instant.

Great calm awaits you. Simply ask.

Jesus, I admit that life sometimes feels like a storm-tossed boat on waves too big to tackle or navigate. I cannot calm the chaos of my heart. I cannot make this work. Please bring peace to my life. Please rescue me. Help. Amen.

DAY FIFTY-NINE
WOMAN WITH THE ISSUE OF BLOOD

She thought, "If I can just touch his robe, I will be healed."
Jesus turned around, and when he saw her he said, "Daughter,
be encouraged! Your faith has made you well." And
the woman was healed at that moment.

MATTHEW 9:21-22

The woman who touches the fringe of Jesus's cloak suffered for 12 years with a debilitating, constant bleeding (Matthew 9:20). Imagine losing blood every single day for 12 years. Imagine the anemia, the weakness—not to mention that because she bled, she had to live on the outskirts of fellowship. "Unclean" was her constant moniker.

Desperation, coupled with the stories she must have heard about Jesus's ability to miraculously heal, propels the woman with the issue of blood. Faith in Jesus causes her pursuit.

She interrupts Jesus on his way to resurrect a 12-year-old girl (Mark 5:42; Luke 8:42). The irony is thick. This girl lived life under the joyful gaze of her parents for 12 years, only to have her life snuffed out. The woman lived life bereft of fellowship for 12 years, spending her time and money pursuing a cure that never materialized (Mark 5:26). Twelve years of life for both, and both would be radically interrupted in the best possible way by the Author of life and healing.

Although Jesus has been stalled on the way to heal a young girl, he calls this sweet, suffering woman a daughter. Such an affectionate, beautiful moniker, isn't it? In calling her that, he welcomes her back into the fold of the living, beckoning toward community. Her exile caused by illness is wonderfully concluded. She is a daughter of the King, and as such, she can eat at the King's table without having to crawl along the cobbled streets to touch the fringe of his garment.

There are two important elements to note about prayer here. One is faith. You must truly believe that Jesus is able to heal, intercede, and help. The other is pursuit. There is no such thing as passive healing. Christianity is active. It involves the sacrifice of pursuit. In pursuit, you are recognizing your own limitations. You cannot help yourself, so you pursue the only One who can.

Pursue God today with belief as your fuel.

Jesus, I choose to believe in your power, your ability to transform a life. Would you see me here on earth? Would you intercede when I cannot? Would you heal me? I want to be a disciple who pursues you first, who sees you as the source of my life. Amen.

DAY SIXTY

Two Blind Men

After Jesus left the girl's home, two blind men followed along
behind him, shouting, "Son of David, have mercy on us!"
They went right into the house where he was staying, and Jesus
asked them, "Do you believe I can make you see?" "Yes, Lord,"
they told him, "we do." Then he touched their eyes and said,
"Because of your faith, it will happen." Then their eyes were
opened, and they could see!

MATTHEW 9:27-30

What would it be like to have no sight? To have to feel your way through life? To open your eyes in the morning only to "see" darkness? This was the daily reality of these blind companions.

How beautiful, first, that they found each other. Togetherness has significance. Together, the two blind men pursued the One known to give sight to the spiritually and physically blind. Although Jesus called the Pharisees "blind guides leading the blind" (Matthew 15:14), these two companions epitomized the opposite of that. Together, they led each other to Jesus.

We need companions like that. We can pray for friends who will walk alongside us when life feels dark and foreboding. We can ask God to provide the kind of daily fellowship our souls crave in this fragmented digital world.

The companionship of these two blind men resulted in a beautiful pursuit. Together, they approached Jesus with boldness. They followed Jesus. Then they shouted.

We, too, have that same opportunity today. We can follow in the footsteps of our Rabbi, the One who teaches all truths, empowers the weak, and dignifies the broken. We can follow him down the dusty roads of our lives with sheer joy, in anticipation of the adventure to which he beckons us. We can exercise the same kind of relentless pursuit these men did—not only following Jesus down a path, but entering a stranger's house to make a request of him.

And when we are wearied by our weakness, we can be like these friends and shout our need. We can approach Jesus with our sicknesses, lack of ability, fears, heartaches, soul-crushing defeats, and powerlessness. And he will hear us. He does not despise our outcry.

Jesus, would you send a companion to walk alongside me in this life? A friend in the storm? Someone who understands my weakness and frailty? And when you provide that person, would you also quicken my heart to be bold enough to follow you wherever you lead me? While I may not shout my requests to you today, I know you hear me even when I whisper my worries. Amen.

DAY SIXTY-ONE

PETER

*When he saw the strong wind and the waves, he was terrified
and began to sink. "Save me, Lord!" he shouted. Jesus
immediately reached out and grabbed him. "You have so little
faith," Jesus said. "Why did you doubt me?"*

MATTHEW 14:30-31

Simon Peter did what most nonswimmers would shrink from—
he stepped onto the water, attempting to walk toward Jesus, who
stood as if he placed his feet on dry ground. The One who created the
law of gravity stood before Peter, defying it spectacularly.

Initially captured by Jesus's beckoning words, Peter—always first
to act, second to think—barged out of the boat. And for a halcyon
moment, he wavered not.

When Jesus asks us to do the seeming impossible, we would be wise
to follow the boisterous example of Peter, to boldly follow the One who
created it all.

But, like Peter, we are prone to wander—especially with our eyes.
Once perfectly fixed on the perfect One, our gazes become captured
by the realities surrounding us. We panic. We sink. We fear. We allow
the waves to obscure our sight.

Peter utters the most guttural prayer: "Save me, Lord!" (Matthew
14:30). In this exclamation, Peter acknowledges his limitations and
points to the limitless Lord. He cannot save himself. He cannot walk
on water, let alone swim. He is in a desperate situation, seesawing
between life and death.

In this request, not only does Peter declare his helplessness, but he reaches out to the One who created every element he could see: the wind, the sky, the waves, the watery depths. Jesus, as Creator, masters the world's elements. He spins the earth on its axis. He cares for birds. He owns the cattle on a thousand hills. He formed mountains. The Creator is best equipped to rescue his creation from the elements.

We, too, follow the One who created everything we see, even the laws, formulas, and theories that govern this world. He is Lord of it all—Lord of the seas, Lord of the land, Lord of the cosmos, Lord of the far-flung galaxies.

Not only does Jesus exercise this kind of awe-inspiring power, but he is also personal. He cares for the individual. When Peter cries out, Jesus rescues him. Although he laments Peter's lack of faith, he does not let the waves overtake the disciple.

Jesus's power is married to personal care. This is something to celebrate today as we pray.

Jesus, help! Save me! I am drowning. I can't save myself. Only you are powerful over the forces of evil I face. Only you command the wind and clouds and sky. Only you created it all. And yet you care for me. I cannot conceive of your kindness. Help me know that you see me today while the waves threaten to panic me. Amen.

DAY SIXTY-TWO

GENTILE WOMAN

*[A Gentile woman] came and worshiped him, pleading again,
"Lord, help me!" Jesus responded, "It isn't right to take food
from the children and throw it to the dogs." She replied, "That's
true, Lord, but even dogs are allowed to eat the scraps that
fall beneath their masters' table." "Dear woman," Jesus said
to her, "your faith is great. Your request is granted." And her
daughter was instantly healed.*

MATTHEW 15:25-28

Upon first reading of this passage, it sounds like Jesus is harsh toward the Gentile woman, but we must remember that Jesus, as a rabbi, is constantly creating teaching moments for the disciples who are a captive audience for this interaction. He wants them to hear her pleas. He wants them to hear his response.

Why? Because God's unfolding plan since the beginning of time was to reconcile an unreconciled humanity to himself—both Jew and Gentile. He had empowered the nation of Israel as a chosen people to proclaim his excellencies to the nations around them. They were to woo others to the covenantal God who loved them too.

But Israel had cherished their specialness to the point that they did not reach outward. They focused on themselves, failing to proclaim God's plan to those outside the commonwealth.

So when Jesus interacts with this Gentile woman, he is training his disciples to expand their view of the kingdom of God. No longer does the word *kingdom* reference a political entity with an earthly king. No, it is a spiritual kingdom made up of all races, both sexes, all strata of people—who bow before a heavenly King.

All of us are beneath our Master's table, receiving from his hand. All of us are included in this great salvation that stretches beyond borders. We have the privilege today not only to pray for those who don't yet know the Lord, but to share the gospel with everyone we meet. This invitation is not for the special ones, the perfect ones (no such ones exist), the insiders. No, this is an invitation to those who call themselves "lost" and "needy."

As you pray for those who are far from God, let Jesus's compassion for every single human being fuel your words. You are doing his work when you look beyond your borders and pray.

Jesus, I pray for those in my circle and those who are far away from me geographically, that you would draw all men and women to yourself. Give me the boldness I need to dare to share your good news with those who desperately need hope. We all need to know that you have welcomed us to your table as your children. Thank you, King Jesus! Amen.

DAY SIXTY-THREE

FATHER

Lord, have mercy on my son. He has seizures and suffers terribly.
He often falls into the fire or into the water. So I brought him to
your disciples, but they couldn't heal him.

MATTHEW 17:15-16

What a powerful picture of fatherly love portrayed in this interaction. The most important thing we can do for our children (whether biological, adopted, or spiritual) is to bring them to Jesus, beseeching him to heal them, comfort them, and set them free.

This boy suffered. And in that suffering, his father faced certain desperation. He did what he could—and it turned out to be the best pursuit, resulting in the healing of his son.

But first he approached the disciples in hopes that they could perform the healing the boy needed. While Jesus did send the disciples (first the 12, then the 70) to minister in the cities surrounding Jerusalem, empowering them to pray, heal, and preach the kingdom, in this case, they could not help the father with his request.

This echoes our own journeys. We often go first to professional men and women to bring healing to our loved ones. While that is normative and correct, our initial response should be to bring the issue to the throne of the Almighty God, asking for wisdom, direction, and help.

In Matthew 17:19-20, the disciples ask, "Why couldn't we cast out that demon?"

"You don't have enough faith," Jesus replies. "I tell you the truth, if you had faith even as small as a mustard seed, you could say to this mountain, 'Move from here to there,' and it would move. Nothing would be impossible."

Today we are blessed with the Holy Spirit, who empowers our faith, emboldens our prayers, and gives shape to our cries. Yes, we may lack faith as the disciples did, but the Spirit within will stir it up. Yes, we may often run to human-made solutions as our knee-jerk reaction, but through the gentle tutelage of the Spirit, we can choose prayer as our first response.

Be assured that God is touched by your pain and the pain of your loved one. He is able to help, ready to listen, powerful to move. When you intercede on behalf of another, particularly a child, you are praying the language of love.

God loves to answer that kind of parental prayer. He, too, is a parent, and as a good Father, he loves to give his children good gifts (Matthew 7:11).

Jesus, I pray for those whom you've entrusted to me, whether they be biological, adoptive, or spiritual children. Would you come alongside those who struggle? Would you heal the brokenhearted? Would you bind up the wounds of those who are far from you? Would you cause them to reach to you? Would you do something new? Amen.

DAY SIXTY-FOUR
Two Blind Men

*Two blind men were sitting beside the road. When they heard
that Jesus was coming that way, they began shouting, "Lord,
Son of David, have mercy on us!" "Be quiet!" the crowd yelled
at them. But they only shouted louder, "Lord, Son of David,
have mercy on us!" When Jesus heard them, he stopped and
called, "What do you want me to do for you?"
"Lord," they said, "we want to see!"*

MATTHEW 20:30-33

In calling Jesus the "Son of David," these two blind men uttered
something profound. "Son of David" is a messianic title. The One
who would finally redeem Israel would come from David's line and
would rule eternally. As the blind men said this, it must have quickened Jesus's joy. They got it. They understood exactly who he was. Their
words were a proclamation of faith.

Assured of who Jesus was, they were able to disregard the peer pressure of the crowd and persevere. They did not let the cries of others
drown out their own. Instead, they allowed the resistance of others to
incite their own shouts.

What powerful lessons. Jesus is moved when we proclaim who he
is as we go about our days. When we call Jesus "the Messiah" in front
of others, we establish that we are his and that he is the Master of
everything.

And when we wholeheartedly pursue Jesus Christ, even to the dismay of those who tell us not to, we exercise our faith like these two
blind men. Know this: When you decide to interact with and follow

Jesus, you will face persecution. There will be friends and family members who will denigrate your pursuit. This is normative. Keep persevering. Do not let the anger or pushback of another thwart your mind-set of following Jesus with everything you have.

Also, take note of the way Jesus interacted with the blind men. He did not assume their response. He invited them into relationship with a question. He asked what they wanted from him. This simple question invited their answer. They wanted mercy from the Son of David. They wanted relief from their Lord. Simply put, they wanted sight.

Jesus, Son of David, the Lord of all creation, granted their faith-infused request. Despite the naysayers all around, Jesus looked intently on them and then granted their sight. They had been blind, but now they could see. And the first person they saw with their healed eyes was the God of all light.

Jesus, help me pursue you with everything I have, despite what others around me say. Help me persevere through persecution. I acknowledge that you are the Son of David, the Messiah who came to take away the sins of the world. Thank you for the example of the blind men who had faith and perseverance. Amen.

DAY SIXTY-FIVE

JESUS

He went on a little farther and bowed with his face to the ground, praying, "My Father! If it is possible, let this cup of suffering be taken away from me. Yet I want your will to be done, not mine."... Then Jesus left them a second time and prayed, "My Father! If this cup cannot be taken away unless I drink it, your will be done."... He went to pray a third time, saying the same things again.

MATTHEW 26:39,42,44

In the Garden of Gethsemane, we see the most anguished prayer recorded in the history of the world. Jesus faces the most excruciating decision—that of death for the sake of reconciling humankind to God.

In his hypostatic union of fully God, fully man, we see the struggle play out as drops of sweat-turned-blood weep from our Savior. He knows the anguish awaiting him. He is well aware of the betrayal to come; the cackle of evil supposedly triumphing over him; the whipping, beating, and cross bearing; the feel of nails pounded into flesh; the impossibility of heaving in another breath. This he knows. This he faces.

And he says yes.

We are here today because of that decision made in prayer in a garden. Humanity rebelled against God in a garden, and the sacred One crushed the serpent on a cross fashioned of wood—a decision finalized in a garden populated by olive trees. What a beautiful bookend.

Though we will never have to face such a monumental decision with so much at stake, we can still model this prayer in our lives. We all have a will and a longing to do things our way, taking the easy way out. To pray "Your will be done" is a faith-filled utterance of spiritual warfare. It's saying no to our selfishness and yes to the way of God.

Our holy, holy, holy Savior prayed this assenting prayer three times, cementing his intent. Yes, empathically, he would die in humanity's place. Yes, he would follow God down the narrow, painful path. Yes, he would sacrifice himself for our sake.

Our response is simply this: worship.

Jesus, I cannot fathom your decision. I love you. I'm indebted to you for your choice. I'm humbled. Grateful. Mindful of your sacrifice. "Thank you" seems utterly small in light of all you've done for me, for them, for us. I worship you today with holy abandon. Amen.

DAY SIXTY-SIX

JESUS

At about three o'clock, Jesus called out with a loud voice,
"Eli, Eli, lema sabachthani?" which means
"My God, my God, why have you abandoned me?"

MATTHEW 27:46

Jesus's last words were a prayer.

The time of day Jesus's crucifixion began and the time when it ended have important significance. Both were typical times of Jewish worship, the 9:00 a.m. hour (when the crucifixion began; Mark 15:25) being the ordinary commencement of morning sacrifices, and the 3:00 p.m. hour (when Jesus died) being a time of prayer. But during the Passover festival, the paschal lamb must be slain beginning at 3:00 p.m. [4] How beautifully Jesus fulfills the Scriptures on multiple levels.

So we see Jesus's death beginning and ending in sacrifice, with the symbolism of his death as a Passover lamb fully intact. Jesus also prayed a prayer from Psalm 22:1. This shows us the power of praying the word of God back to God, and it also helped onlookers and witnesses make important connections about the true identity of Jesus.

Psalm 22 is a messianic psalm. Consider:

> I am a worm and not a man. I am scorned and despised by all! Everyone who sees me mocks me. They sneer and shake their heads, saying, "Is this the one who relies on the LORD? Then let the LORD save him! If the LORD loves him so much, let the LORD rescue him!" (verses 6-8).

My enemies surround me like a pack of dogs; an evil gang
closes in on me. They have pierced my hands and feet. I
can count all my bones. My enemies stare at me and gloat.
They divide my garments among themselves and throw
dice for my clothing (verses 16-18).

Written lifetimes before Jesus walked the earth, these very words of
David are fulfilled between 9:00 a.m. and 3:00 p.m. by Jesus Christ in
startling clarity on the day of his crucifixion.

Jesus cried out to God at the hour of prayer. His prayer was honest, full of angst and agony. For in this holy moment, God the Father,
from whom Jesus had never once experienced separation, had to turn
away from his Son as he bore the weight of all of humankind's sin—all
in anticipation of future victory.

Not only can we pray our agonies like Jesus did, but we also will
never have to experience the abandonment of God because of what
he accomplished on the cross. In Psalm 22:27, we see the outcome of
Jesus's radical obedience: "The whole earth will acknowledge the LORD
and return to him. All the families of the nations will bow down before
him." We are those families!

Jesus, how can I thank you for your sacrifice, my dear Passover
Lamb who takes away the sins of the world? Thank you for laying
down your life for me. Thank you that your final words were prayer.
Teach me to pray everything, including my agony—in authenticity.
Thank you for making a way for me. Amen.

DAY SIXTY-SEVEN

SIMEON

Sovereign Lord, now let your servant die in peace, as you have promised. I have seen your salvation, which you have prepared for all people. He is a light to reveal God to the nations, and he is the glory of your people Israel!

LUKE 2:29-32

Simeon said these words when he first laid eyes on Jesus. We now have the privilege to learn from Simeon and his heart for prayer. We discover in earlier verses that Simeon lived in Jerusalem. He was known to be devout, and he constantly hoped and prayed for the Messiah to come. He'd had such a close relationship with God that he'd heard directly from the Holy Spirit that he would not die until he saw the Messiah with his own aging eyes. So Simeon, old in years but strong in hope, waited. And waited. And waited some more.

In that anticipation, Mary and Joseph brought Jesus to the temple to be dedicated. God's perfectly timed plan. The Scripture says that Simeon took Jesus in his arms and then declared his prayer of blessing over the Messiah. Mary and Joseph stood stunned at the proclamation of truth about their son. Jesus would be the one to rescue both Israelites and Gentiles to God Almighty—the true essence of the gospel.

The man who heard the voice of the third person of the Trinity now held the second member of the Trinity in his arms. And as he did, he prayed to the first person of the Trinity—declaring the beautiful truth of God the Father's power and his indelible plan of salvation for all the nations. Simeon calls God "sovereign"—the ruler of all, the One who always has a plan, though his people may have wondered when his global plan would finally come to pass.

We learn from Simeon that God is faithful. He delivers on his promises. He answers prayers.

But there's still more to this narrative. Simeon, empowered by the Spirit, prophesies further over the Son. He tells Mary, "This child is destined to cause many in Israel to fall, and many others to rise. He has been sent as a sign from God, but many will oppose him. As a result, the deepest thoughts of many hearts will be revealed. And a sword will pierce your very soul" (Luke 2:34-35).

Snuck into Simeon's words is a warning for us all. When we encounter Jesus Christ, he reveals what's in our hearts—the good, the wayward, the lamenting, as well as the hope. The very nature of Jesus lays us bare, but just as Simeon beheld Jesus in his arms, we also have the privilege of looking into his face. Like Simeon, we are lost in the mystery of it all, captivated by the stunning intersection of God with humanity—in order to save us all.

Jesus, thank you for answering the long-standing prayers of Simeon in such a powerful way. Empower me to pray daring prayers like that, to anticipate your salvation not only in my life, but also in the lives of others. I want to be so close to your Spirit that I know his voice and instantly obey. Amen.

DAY SIXTY-EIGHT
RICH MAN

*The rich man shouted, "Father Abraham, have some pity! Send
Lazarus over here to dip the tip of his finger in water and cool
my tongue. I am in anguish in these flames." But Abraham
said to him, "Son, remember that during your lifetime you had
everything you wanted, and Lazarus had nothing. So now he is
here being comforted, and you are in anguish. And besides, there
is a great chasm separating us. No one can cross over to you from
here, and no one can cross over to us from there."*

LUKE 16:24-26

While not a prayer, per se, this scene is part of a parable told by
Jesus about the finality of death and the importance of how
we live our lives on earth.

We see an unnamed rich man who lived lavishly on earth, not even
giving the poor man scraps from his table. But the poor man (named
Lazarus) spent his time in abject poverty at the gate of the rich man,
with open sores attended to by dogs that licked his wounds. Knowing
the way Jewish people viewed dogs (as unclean), this was a desperate
spot indeed. The man had been so weakened by his state that he lacked
the motivation to shoo the dogs away.

Both men die, and one is relieved of suffering, while the other
begins his agony.

We see the ineffectiveness of prayer after death. Though the rich
man pleads with Abraham, he is rebuked. He cannot turn around and
make a change in his life. He cannot repent of his actions. He cannot
change the outcome of his tormented state.

This serves as a poignant reminder to us all. We have a short stint on this earth, and how we live and reach out to God matters. Spending a life in dependence through prayer enables us to know God and the ways of his kingdom now. We currently have the opportunity to follow Jesus on the narrow way, a passage toward God that few find (see Matthew 7:13-14). One nanosecond after we die, we will see everything quite clearly—what we regret not doing and what we regret doing.

Scripture says we should make the most of our time here on earth because our days are evil (Ephesians 5:16).

The point of this passage is not that rich people can't enter heaven and poor people are always rewarded with eternal blessings. It's that one of these people chose to live life apart from Jesus, and the other did not. This stark reality should not only fuel our prayers for those who are far from God, but also inform the way we choose to live today.

Jesus, I pray for the "rich" people in my life who believe they have no need of you. Help them understand the finality of death, the reality of the afterlife, and the necessity to pray to you for rescue. In light of this passage, help me understand more deeply the fleeting nature of my life. I want to follow you down the narrow way. Amen.

DAY SIXTY-NINE
TEN LEPERS

Ten men with leprosy stood at a distance, crying out, "Jesus, Master, have mercy on us!" He looked at them and said, "Go show yourselves to the priests." And as they went, they were cleansed of their leprosy. One of them, when he saw that he was healed, came back to Jesus, shouting, "Praise God!" He fell to the ground at Jesus' feet, thanking him for what he had done. This man was a Samaritan.

LUKE 17:12-16

Ten leprous men cried out for relief from their skin condition. Scripture says they did this from a distance. They knew their place. Unclean people could not participate in the community life of Israel. So they shouted from afar.

Jesus had mercy upon them, healing all ten as they ventured toward the priests. Nine continued on with their lives, not even stopping to revel in the marvel that had just happened. Nine failed to return to Jesus to thank him for his miraculous intervention. He had utterly transformed them, from leprous to pink skinned, from outcasts to insiders, from despised to welcomed, from rejected to revered as healed people.

They simply continued on.

But one man could not.

He stopped, marveled, then turned. He found Jesus. He shouted praises. He bowed. He thanked him. This man gave glory to the One who healed him.

Interestingly, Jesus asserts something at which his audience would balk. He knew the nationality of the one who returned—a Samaritan, a hated race. The implication in Luke 17:18 is that the other nine were of pure Jewish descent, but they failed to return to give thanks: "Has no one returned to give glory to God except this foreigner?" They treated Jesus as if he were any other person, no big deal. Theirs was a callous dismissal.

When we pray, we can also be like this Samaritan Jesus praised. We can stop, turn around, and return to him to thank him for all he has done. Our lives are busy, yes. But when we continue on without thanking God for our breath, our life, the beauty that is our relationships, the provisions he gives, we forsake our God.

He deserves the pause. He deserves the return. He deserves the kneeling. He deserves the praise.

Oh, to slow down enough to really appreciate the miraculous things God has done! To realize it is sheer disobedience to move forward without first thanking him.

> Jesus, I choose today to pause, to stop, to reflect, and then to return to you to thank you for all you have done. I don't want to be like the nine lepers who nonchalantly neglected to thank you. You are my healer. You are my strength. Everything I have comes from your hand. Oh, how I thank you. Amen.

DAY SEVENTY
Pharisee and Tax Collector

*The Pharisee stood by himself and prayed this prayer: "I thank
you, God, that I am not like other people—cheaters, sinners,
adulterers. I'm certainly not like that tax collector! I fast twice
a week, and I give you a tenth of my income." But the tax
collector stood at a distance and dared not even lift his eyes
to heaven as he prayed. Instead, he beat his chest in sorrow,
saying, "O God, be merciful to me, for I am a sinner." I tell
you, this sinner, not the Pharisee, returned home justified
before God. For those who exalt themselves will be humbled,
and those who humble themselves will be exalted.*

LUKE 18:11-14

In this parable, the Pharisee's prayer is a clear example of how *not* to
pray. The tax collector's prayer is a beautiful model of how *to* pray.

In the first prayer, we see the Pharisee standing aloof from others,
not because he feels that he must remove himself in piety, but because
of his high opinion of himself and the need to remove himself from
the rabble. His first word in the prayer is *I*. In fact, count the number
of times *I* appears in the Pharisee's prayer. Five times he refers to himself. Instead of praying, his words are praise choruses to his own magnanimous ways. His identity? Sinlessness (apparently). He is a citizen
who is morally upright, one who fasts and tithes. His only thanks to
God reflect his own personal greatness. His prayer is boasting, arro-
gant, prideful.

But the tax collector approaches God with humility. His prayer
starts with humble action. His standing at a distance does not arise

from pride, but agony. He knows he needs grace. He knows his unworthiness before a holy God. He won't even lift his gaze heavenward. He pounds upon himself. He exemplifies godly sorriness. The first two words of his prayer are "O God." He appeals to God's mercy and calls himself a sinner.

In a nutshell, Jesus warns us not to exalt ourselves, saying that if we do, we will be humbled. And if we choose the path of the tax collector—that of humility—we will find exaltation.

Our prayers don't have to be full of elaborate words in an attempt to prove our worthiness to our worthy God. He loves us. We are his children. We have no need to boast except in what he has done for us. In the midst of trials or strife, we can simply start our prayers with God, asking for his mercy, reminding him of our state without him.

This is the true essence of prayer. To be humble. To praise the worthy One. To acknowledge our state without Jesus. To trust in his ample mercy.

Jesus, have mercy upon me, a sinner. I have nothing to offer you except my gratitude and humility. I choose to humble myself before you, knowing that you will raise me at the proper time. In the meantime, I rest in knowing the One who is worthy instills worth in me, not because of anything I've done, but because of who you are and whose I am. Amen.

DAY SEVENTY-ONE
OFFICIAL

The official pleaded, "Lord, please come now before my little boy dies." Then Jesus told him, "Go back home. Your son will live!" And the man believed what Jesus said and started home.

JOHN 4:49-50

This father was known as an official. He had high ranking. No doubt he was accustomed to making requests of powerful people and having them hop to help him. But in this interaction with Jesus, we see something different. This official pleaded. There's desperation lacing his request as his little boy faces death. He is a desperate parent.

His request? *Please come to my house. Touch my son. Heal him.* No doubt he had heard of the power that came from the hands of Jesus.

But note what Jesus said to the official. He refused the man's request! He would not follow the man back home. He would not lay his hands upon the son's feverish brow. He would not utter words of healing or lift him back to life. No, he told the father to return to his home.

And the father obeyed.

He did not argue with Jesus. He did not demand that Jesus be physically there to heal his son. He simply obeyed. Jesus told him to return home, and so he did.

The Christian life is actually quite simple. Plead to Jesus in prayer. Listen to his words, then obey them, whether they make sense or not. We try to complicate things. But we must remember that obedience is what God desires of us more than anything else. This man began his time with pleading prayer and ended it with a healed son.

We must be cautious of prescribing to God the way he must answer our prayers. This man began his prayer this prescriptive way, but he was also flexible. When Jesus decided to heal a different way, the man allowed for Jesus's creativity. He gave room for the miraculous in a new and surprising way.

We sometimes get angry with God because we pray in a specific manner. We ask God to act in a particular way, and when our wildly creative God doesn't answer according to the pathway we have prescribed, we get angry that our expectations aren't met.

Instead, like this father, we must be flexible, then obedient. We must let God answer in his way, his timing, his method. It may differ from last time. We must not make our experience of God in the past into the idol we worship today.

Jesus, I love you. I am grateful for you. I'm thankful that you operate in different ways. Help me hold loosely the way you answer my prayers. I give you space to be creative. And as you speak to me, I want to be a follower who obeys you, even if your commands don't always make sense to me. Amen.

DAY SEVENTY-TWO

JESUS

*They rolled the stone aside. Then Jesus looked up to heaven and
said, "Father, thank you for hearing me. You always hear me,
but I said it out loud for the sake of all these people standing
here, so that they will believe you sent me." Then Jesus shouted,
"Lazarus, come out!" And the dead man came out, his hands
and feet bound in graveclothes, his face wrapped in a headcloth.
Jesus told them, "Unwrap him and let him go!"*

JOHN 11:41-44

This prayer of resurrection changes everything in Jesus's ministry. While the Pharisees are frustrated with him, battling jealousy and an internal rage, it is this miracle of raising Lazarus to life that
cements them against Jesus (see John 11:45-53). This resurrection ush-
ers in the death of Jesus.

Jesus must know this, but he chooses to resurrect his friend come
what may.

Jesus says this prayer aloud so others could record it and we could
read it. He calls God "Father." This reveals his sonship. He thanks
his Father for hearing him, then he mentions that the Father always
hears him. In an intimate relationship between child and parent,
this makes sense. A parent in close proximity hears the pleas of his or
her child. This is normative.

His next words are not mild or hesitant. They seep authority. With
a shout, Jesus commands his dear friend to come out from the grave.

Jesus is Lord of the living and the dead. He is the conqueror of
death. He commands the world and all its elements. In this radical

resurrection, he shows the entire cosmos that he is indeed God, and that God is in him. The Spirit within him empowers him as well, revealing the triune nature of God in one unmistakable miracle.

Sometimes we forget the power of Jesus. We forget that he can do anything. He can defy the laws of our physical world. He created resurrection. He *is* the resurrection.

In light of that, our prayers take on a more important role. We are communing with the God of everything, the God who can make the dead dance. He is a God who speaks life over his children. He hears us. He is intimately connected to us. He loves to answer our requests. And he is powerful, so powerful.

When we pray, let us remember Lazarus and this moment that Jesus undertook at great risk to himself. This act led to the cross, where Jesus chose to bear the weight of sin upon his sinless self.

Lazarus eventually died. But death could not hold Jesus. He is risen even now.

Jesus, wow! You are powerful. You have conquered death. You have been permanently raised to life through power. You are greater than me, greater than my small strength. Would you empower me to pray bold prayers? Help me remember how great you are. Amen.

DAY SEVENTY-THREE

JESUS

Now my soul is deeply troubled. Should I pray,
"Father, save me from this hour"? But this is the very
reason I came! Father, bring glory to your name.

JOHN 12:27-28

We see the agony of Jesus in this prayer. This interaction with his disciples comes on the heels of his triumphant entry into Jerusalem, where people chanted praises to him, revering him. He must have understood that their fickle faith would soon turn to cruel crucifixion with their next breath.

They praised him because they'd seen the miraculous, and they were curious. Jesus, to them, was a commodity at which to gawk. "Many in the crowd had seen Jesus call Lazarus from the tomb, raising him from the dead, and they were telling others about it. That was the reason so many went out to meet him—because they had heard about this miraculous sign" (John 12:17-18).

As mentioned yesterday, this miracle prompted Jesus's demise. "The Pharisees said to each other, 'There's nothing we can do. Look, everyone has gone after him!'" (verse 19). After all this, some Greeks (friends of Philip) met with Jesus alongside his disciples. Jesus then uttered these bittersweet words: "Now the time has come for the Son of Man to enter into his glory. I tell you the truth, unless a kernel of wheat is planted in the soil and dies, it remains alone. But its death will produce many new kernels—a plentiful harvest of new lives" (verses 23-24).

After this, he mentions his troubled soul and asks if he should pray to God to save him from his fate. In this space, he chooses not to beseech God, but to declare his obedience. That, too, is prayer. To walk without hesitation in obedience, to bring glory not to your own name, but to God's—that is prayer.

God's response to Jesus's obedience in prayer is this: "I have already brought glory to my name, and I will do so again" (verse 28). The onlookers believe that they heard thunder instead or that an angel responded to Jesus (verse 29). And even though they experienced this profound miracle, they continue to question Jesus about death. Why would the Messiah die? Wouldn't he vanquish the evil Roman Empire and live eternally?

How difficult it must have been for our Lord to endure this subtle and not-so-subtle undermining of his plan. How easy it would have been to choose life over death, to circumvent the agony of the cross.

But he chose the cross. And because he did so, we can now freely enter into relationship with the Godhead—the Father, Son, and Holy Spirit. He did not bow to the flattery or ease of others. No, his prayer was his obedience. As followers of Jesus, ours should be the same.

Jesus, thank you for choosing to listen only to the voice of your Father as you ventured toward the cross. Thank you for choosing to glorify him over taking the easy way around. You did not circumvent the cross, but rather endured it. In light of that, help me choose to follow you, obey you, and worship you. Amen.

DAY SEVENTY-FOUR

JESUS

*After saying all these things, Jesus looked up to heaven and
said, "Father, the hour has come. Glorify your Son so he can
give glory back to you. For you have given him authority
over everyone. He gives eternal life to each one you have
given him. And this is the way to have eternal life—to
know you, the only true God, and Jesus Christ, the one
you sent to earth. I brought glory to you here on earth by
completing the work you gave me to do. Now, Father, bring
me into the glory we shared before the world began."*

JOHN 17:1-5

In this high priestly prayer, Jesus again shares with his disciples how
to pray through demonstration. In this prayer, he preaches the gospel, the good news of the kingdom. There is much to unpack from his
profound words.

Time is in God's hands. We may not know epochs or eras, but we
can rest our lives in the One who holds it all.

Glory is reverence and light. To glorify is to highlight the greatness of another. Jesus glorified the Father, and the Father returned the
favor. This points to their divinity, revealing a little more of the triune
nature of God.

Jesus has authority. Over everyone. He chooses to give eternal life
to those he has called. Because of this, we must live our lives in worship of him. Because we have the privilege of knowing him, we revel
in that privilege.

Jesus reminds us that eternal life does not begin after we take our last earthly breath, but rather the moment we meet him. And our goal should be to know the God who saved us. That is the essence of life itself—to know God. Not only to be known by him, but to press on to know his heartbeat.

Jesus brought the Father glory by doing what the Father placed before him. And we can do the same. Oh, for us to declare like Jesus, "I brought glory to you here on earth by completing the work you gave me to do" (John 17:4). We have a lifetime to achieve the task God has placed before us, but the time is fleeting. Our job is to discover God's will, then obey it with everything inside us.

Finally, Jesus reiterates that he was with God the Father in creation. They, along with the Holy Spirit, fashioned our world, this universe, the stars, the seas, the mountains, the atoms from nothing—all by speaking them into existence. Because of this, we live in utter reverence of our triune, creative God.

Jesus, I want to complete the work you have called me to do. Help me glorify you as you glorified the Father, by shedding light on your goodness in my life. Thank you for creating the world. Thank you for the mystery of the Trinity. Thank you for saving me. Amen.

DAY SEVENTY-FIVE

JESUS

*My prayer is not for the world, but for those you have given me,
because they belong to you. All who are mine belong to you, and
you have given them to me, so they bring me glory. Now I am
departing from the world; they are staying in this world, but I
am coming to you. Holy Father, you have given me your name;
now protect them by the power of your name so that they will be
united just as we are. During my time here, I protected them by
the power of the name you gave me. I guarded them so that not
one was lost, except the one headed for destruction,
as the Scriptures foretold.*

JOHN 17:9-12

As Jesus continues his high priestly prayer, he prays for us! In this
moment of history, he prays for all he would call his own, which
includes all of us who have followed him down the narrow path. What
a privilege!

His heart is that we bring him glory. To bring glory to him is to
obey him without hesitation and to acknowledge his powerful role in
our lives.

Jesus often prepared the disciples for his death, and in this prayer,
he does so again, saying he will be returning to his Father soon. He will
be leaving this world, and as he does, he will conquer evil upon the
cross, then rise to life again, ever living to intercede for us (see Hebrews
7:24-25). This prayer is continued to this day, as he never ceases to pray
for us even now.

Jesus prays for protection for his disciples and all who will follow him. He calls upon the name of God the Father, the character of the One who fathers his children beautifully. By that name, we are protected. We are sealed. We are loved. We are pursued. We are cherished. We are forgiven. We are set free. We are given hope.

Jesus prays for deep unity—the kind that exists in perfect relationship between the members of our triune God. God the Father, God the Son, and God the Holy Spirit have existed in self-giving love forever. They are the epitome of perfection in relationship, and if we are to represent God well, we, as his followers, must also live in unity.

Here Jesus alludes to Judas, a disciple he poured his life into even though he knew that Judas would hand him over to be crucified. Jesus, knowing full well the nature of Judas, still chose to love him until the end. Oh, to love like that!

Jesus, I'm afraid to pray for unity. I have some relationships in my life that are shattered and broken. Teach me what I need to do on my part to make things right. Thank you for the example of loving Judas. Give me that kind of supernatural love for my enemies. Would you continue to protect me from the evil in this world as I endeavor to bring glory to your name? Amen.

DAY SEVENTY-SIX

JESUS

*Now I am coming to you. I told them many things while I was
with them in this world so they would be filled with my joy. I
have given them your word. And the world hates them because
they do not belong to the world, just as I do not belong to the
world. I'm not asking you to take them out of the world, but
to keep them safe from the evil one. They do not belong to this
world any more than I do. Make them holy by your truth; teach
them your word, which is truth. Just as you sent me into the
world, I am sending them into the world. And I give myself as a
holy sacrifice for them so they can be made holy by your truth.*

JOHN 17:13-19

As Jesus continues his high priestly prayer, he both teaches and
prays. You can almost hear the urgency in his voice, knowing his
time on earth is short, and he must squeeze everything into a teaching opportunity for the disciples who will be momentarily left behind.

His intent? That the disciples would be filled with joy. This is an
ironic prayer, as the disciples are facing an uncertain future. This is
the power of God at work. Only God can provide a believer that elusive state of joy when the world quakes beneath them. Only God can
steady a follower when everything falls apart. Since he holds all things
together (see Colossians 1:17), he can hold *us* together when life turns
tumultuous.

Jesus intercedes for his followers, which include us, with an impas-
sioned heart. He wants us to understand our precarious position, as
being rooted to this world, yet pulled forward by God's ever-expanding

kingdom. Here we carry on his mission of banishing evil, finding justice, and praying for those who are broken by others.

This all comes through the word of God, which enlightens us. The truth, Jesus reminds us in John 8:32, will set us free. So, while we are tethered to this earth, we are freed by truth. And that emancipating truth compels us to be carriers of light in this dark, lie-entrenched world.

We can pray a similar prayer, asking God to enlighten us, to remind us daily that we are on a mission, though our home is not this earth. We can ask him to protect us from the evil one and the systems of this world that threaten to slow us down or derail us.

Because it is true that as we live in this world, sin can stain us, slow us down, and take our hearts down paths we do not intend to travel.

But we can press into the word of God, seeking the rightness there, saturating ourselves in the truth so that the lies of this world become obvious.

Jesus, in this difficult world, help me remember I am actually not of this world. Give me the strength to live in this world, joyfully carrying out the mission you have set before me. May your word nestle into my heart so I can easily discern truth from lie. And be with me as I sojourn here, bringing me joy in the journey. Amen.

DAY SEVENTY-SEVEN

JESUS

*Father, I want these whom you have given me to be with me
where I am. Then they can see all the glory you gave me because
you loved me even before the world began! O righteous
Father, the world doesn't know you, but I do;
and these disciples know you sent me.*

JOHN 17:24-25

What a profound prayer by Jesus on behalf of his followers!
Keep in mind that he prays these words while the disciples
listen—otherwise, how would they be recorded in Scripture? To boldly
pray, "Jesus, I want to be with you where you are," is to pray that
you'll walk in his footsteps. To pray these daring words means to spend
time watching Jesus in the Gospels, seeing how he interacted with people when he walked the earth.

This prayer echoes these words of Peter in 1 Peter 2:21: "God called
you to do good, even if it means suffering, just as Christ suffered for
you. He is your example, and you must follow in his steps."

To follow in his steps, to be where he is, means welcoming the broken, the outcast, those on the fringes of society. It means doing good,
taking breaks into the wilderness to pray, being concerned for the welfare of those who suffer.

Jesus gave us an example of suffering. He spent himself for the sake
of others. He spent himself for you, for us, by fixing his pursuit on Jerusalem, where crucifixion awaited him. Although innocent, he suffered
at the hands of angry people. Silent before accusations, he truly was the
Lamb of God, slain for all.

Jesus's days during his earthly ministry were spent pouring words into his disciples and followers and demonstrating, with power, that the kingdom of God had come to earth. In like manner, we are to make disciples of all nations, pouring words into the people God places on our pathways, praying for power when we feel (or are) weak. We are to humbly rely on the One who made everything we see, preferring his glory to our own.

If we want to be where Jesus is today, we will find camaraderie alongside those who hurt, who are broken and spilled out. We find Jesus as we serve the least, the last, and the lost. It's a paradox, and it has very little to do with creating our own personal kingdoms and everything to do with partnering with others to build God's invisible, upside-down kingdom.

Let's pray for insight, particularly asking that we will continue to understand that Jesus came from the Father, and now we are sent in his stead, empowered by the Holy Spirit within us to accomplish often unseen and unapplauded work.

Jesus, I want to be where you are. I want to love the unlovely, seek the lost, bear the burden of those who struggle. But I know I am not capable of all this on my own. I desperately need you to help me love this way. Open my eyes to the needs all around me. Teach me the joy of being spilled out for the sake of others and your kingdom. Amen.

DAY SEVENTY-EIGHT

PETER

*Peter said, "I don't have any silver or gold for you. But I'll give
you what I have. In the name of Jesus Christ the Nazarene, get
up and walk!" Then Peter took the lame man by the right hand
and helped him up. And as he did, the man's feet and ankles
were instantly healed and strengthened. He jumped up, stood
on his feet, and began to walk! Then, walking, leaping, and
praising God, he went into the Temple with them.*

ACTS 3:6-8

This interaction with the lame man began with prayer. Peter and
John had just trekked to the temple at 3:00 p.m., the hour of
prayer. In that sacred pursuit, they met this man who had never walked;
he had experienced lameness since birth (Acts 3:1-3).

He sought Peter and John not because of their prayer lives, but
because of a lesser view of God. His highest request wasn't restoration,
but maintenance—to be supplied with the resources necessary to make
it another day.

Peter responded with a prayer-command, invoking the name of
Jesus Christ. This bold proclamation was followed by Peter offering
his hand, pulling the no-longer-lame man to his feet, while Jesus's
name fully healed and restored the man. Imagine the surprise! The
man thought he needed money, but God provided a miracle instead.

His response was certainly not sedate. Testing his feet, ankles, and
legs, he began by walking, but he did not stop there. Leaping replaced
pacing. And soon a dance of utter joy overtook him.

We can learn much from this story.

First, God's power is real. Our prayers, often, are more sedate in nature. *Please give me money. Please give me this, or that, or this.* But perhaps we have forgotten that God has the power and ability to do much more than we even ask (see Ephesians 3:20). We can approach our God with boldness and confidence in light of his very real power.

Second, the name of Jesus Christ has power. When you're overwhelmed, tired, confused, broken, or simply have no words to pray, saying the name of Jesus has power. Not in an incantation, but in beseeching his help.

Third, our response to an answered prayer is important. We must stop. Experience it. Embrace the work of God. And then flat out praise God. The lame man walked, leapt, and danced his praise. He cared nothing for propriety. His frenzy was the result of pure joy and gratitude. We must show the same.

Jesus, help me pray bold prayers. I don't want to settle for asking for small things; I want to approach you with anticipation for the power you provide. Teach me today not to take your answers lightly, but to rejoice at your presence in my life, the provision you give, and the kindness you have so lavishly poured out on me. I want to dance my joy today. Amen.

DAY SEVENTY-NINE

BELIEVERS

"Now, O Lord, hear their threats, and give us, your servants, great boldness in preaching your word. Stretch out your hand with healing power; may miraculous signs and wonders be done through the name of your holy servant Jesus." After this prayer, the meeting place shook, and they were all filled with the Holy Spirit. Then they preached the word of God with boldness.

ACTS 4:29-31

This powerful prayer helped inaugurate the church. Note how Christ-centered the new believers' words are. They do not ask for rescue. They do not ask for provision. They do not ask that God would vanquish their very real enemies.

No. They pray for boldness in preaching the word of God. They ask that God would grace them with his healing power. They ask for miracles, not for their sake, but for the sake of the forward momentum of the kingdom of God. They ask that Jesus be glorified, not them.

It is no wonder that the place shook at the conclusion of their prayer. Their unselfish, faith-infused prayer resulted in a dynamic outpouring of the Holy Spirit.

Note how God swiftly answered their prayer. They asked for boldness, then they immediately received that boldness through the Spirit and continued preaching the word of God to a world desperate for good news.

While it is normative to pray for our personal requests, laying our hearts before our Creator, prayer takes kingdom shape when we move beyond personal intercession toward kingdom pursuit. These are

171

dangerous prayers offered to an untamed God who loves to come to the aid of those who dare to pray such things.

Let this prayer infuse you with daring. May you elevate your prayer language to that of a daily bold request.

Lord, make me bold. Lord, take note of what my enemies are saying and doing. Lord, bring healing to this world. Lord, give me a heart and fearlessness to share your story and word with those who don't yet know you. Lord, may whatever you do through me be because of the powerful Spirit within me. Lord, I choose to give you the glory for whatever work you perform through me. Lord, I am merely a vessel. You are the splendid power within me.

Growing deeper in our prayer lives is possible, and it happens through daily practice, learning to talk to him throughout every day. And as you grow this muscle, you will grow more and more accustomed to making impossible requests of the God of possibility.

Jesus, would you embolden my prayers? Lift my rhetoric beyond my own personal requests to deeper, harder things. I pray you would empower me to share your word with the world outside my door. I trust you to answer this in your perfect timing. Shake my heart of complacency, I pray. Amen.

DAY EIGHTY

STEPHEN

As they stoned him, Stephen prayed, "Lord Jesus, receive my spirit." He fell to his knees, shouting, "Lord, don't charge them with this sin!" And with that, he died.

ACTS 7:59-60

Stephen, the deacon who had just shared the entire history of Israel in narrative, culminating in the good news of Jesus Christ, prayed this prayer of surrender. Prior to this utterance, we see something utterly stunning.

The Jewish leaders were full of rage, shaking their fists at Stephen, who accused them of murdering Jesus. "But Stephen, full of the Holy Spirit, gazed steadily into heaven and saw the glory of God, and he saw Jesus standing in the place of honor at God's right hand. And he told them, 'Look, I see the heavens opened and the Son of Man standing in the place of honor at God's right hand!'" (Acts 7:55-56).

Much like the way we rise when a musical performance is powerful, Jesus, who is normally seated at the right hand of the Father (see Luke 22:69), stands to welcome Stephen to heaven. Stephen endured such hostility with such grace that his welcome resembles an ovation.

Lest we stay lost in this beautiful thought, we must look at the second half of Stephen's prayer, where he mimics Jesus's heart. He asks that God would not charge the Jewish leaders with this sin. Interestingly, Saul, who would later meet Jesus on the road to Damascus (Acts 9), stands right there (Acts 7:58; 8:1). God would beautifully answer Stephen's prayer in Saul-turned-Paul's life. The one who applauds

Stephen's murder would eventually bow before the One who stood at Stephen's homecoming.

From the cross, Jesus uttered, "Father, forgive them, for they don't know what they are doing" (Luke 23:34). Stephen's faith-infused words echo that same sentiment. This reveals that Jesus is not against humanity, but for it. And his mission is to reconcile all men, even enemies of the cross, to himself.

Similarly, we can pray that the Lord would receive our lives. We can lay ourselves bare before the One who knows all things. We can joyfully surrender our hearts to the One who fashioned them. And when we suffer at the hands of others, we can ask God not to count their sin against them. This is a faith-filled, godly prayer. It hints at reconciliation, forgiveness, and the power of God to transform even the most hardened person.

That Saul-turned-Paul eventually helped spread the gospel to the entire known world is telling of the power of grace in the life of a believer. This should encourage us to keep praying for those who are lost. If the apostle Paul, who gloated at Stephen's death, could be transformed, God's power can also change the lives of those we love who are far from him.

Jesus, I surrender. I give you my life. Take it. Do something beautiful from the scraps of my life. Be my strength. I pray for those who are far from you, that you would not hold their sin against them, but forgive them, transforming them into disciples who change the world. Help me trust that you are able to do such a miracle, God. Amen.

DAY EIGHTY-ONE

SAUL

"Who are you, lord?" Saul asked. And the voice replied, "I am Jesus, the one you are persecuting! Now get up and go into the city, and you will be told what you must do."

ACTS 9:5-6

This is one of the most profound prayers we can pray: *Who are you, Lord?*

Jesus was with God the Father and the Holy Spirit before the world and universe were spun into existence. He has always existed. He has no beginning, no end. He is the Son of God and the Son of Man. He appeared to a few as a theophany in the Old Testament. And when the time was ripe, God the Father sent him to earth to be born of a virgin in the town of Bethlehem.

His birth fulfilled many prophecies—his life, death, and resurrection too. He lived in relative obscurity most of his life, living the mundane, learning carpentry. We see a glimpse of his intelligence at age 12, when he stayed behind in Jerusalem—at his Father's house, the temple—teaching and astounding the religious leaders.

He began his ministry through baptism, and God the Father shouted his adoration, while the Holy Spirit descended as a dove. After the pinnacle of that proclamation, he was led into the wilderness, from waters to desert, in the same manner of the Israelites in the exodus. And there he met the ancient foe, Satan, who tempted him toward power, pride, and accumulation. While Satan twisted Scripture, Jesus knew it and rightly interpreted it.

He chose 12 disciples, though one would betray him. Many followed him, including a large contingent of women who funded his ministry (see Luke 8:1-3). He had no place to lay his head. He commanded nature. He healed many diseases, some existing from birth. He verbally wrangled with the religious elite, who were so bent toward jealousy that they plotted to kill him.

Jesus conquered evil. Everywhere evil spirits were, they recoiled in torment at his presence and had to flee. He loved the outcast, noticed the broken, dignified the children, and fed the 5,000, then the 4,000. He toppled tables in the temple, enraged that prayer had become more business than practice. He told stories. He lived the greatest story ever. He retreated from the world to pray to the One who sustained him.

He set his face like flint toward Jerusalem. The fickle ones who shouted, "Hosanna," would later incant, "Crucify." He didn't speak when mocked and condemned, didn't defend himself. Nails pierced his hands and feet, but love and justice held him on the cross for us all. Sin's darkness fell upon the earth when he cried words of forgiveness and surrendered his spirit. It was finished.

Death held him three days in the womb of the earth, but the quaking of life silenced the cackling of the powers of darkness. Sunday morning erupted in light, and the crucified One became the glorified, living Savior. This is Jesus. The One we worship.

Jesus, there are no words. You are good. You are beautiful. You are everything. You are my life. You have saved me. You have redeemed my life from the pit. You have conquered sin and death. You have satisfied justice. You are love. I love you. Amen.

DAY EIGHTY-TWO

PETER

Peter asked them all to leave the room; then he knelt and prayed. Turning to the body he said, "Get up, Tabitha." And she opened her eyes! When she saw Peter, she sat up! He gave her his hand and helped her up. Then he called in the widows and all the believers, and he presented her to them alive.

ACTS 9:40-41

Tabitha, also known as Dorcas, was a woman who loved people well. She had provided for others out of the abundance of her kindness. When she died, she left behind a grieving community. This was precisely the point when the apostle Peter entered the picture. He cleared the room.

There was nothing he could do in his own power to bring life to a dead woman. Nothing in himself that could resurrect a cold body. So he knelt. In that posture of humility, he recognized that he was incapable of bringing a solution to the grieving community. While kneeling, he prayed, asking God to have mercy on this dear woman and her friends.

Only after kneeling and praying did he issue the command for Tabitha to arise. The first thing she did, Scripture tells us, is open her eyes. It doesn't say she took in breath, or sang, or moved her hand. No, she opened her eyes. How thrilling and terrifying that must have been!

Immediately, she sat up. Peter then lifted her to her feet. In death, she reclined. In life, she stood. Resurrection changes everything.

When we come to God on behalf of others, or even on behalf of ourselves, we need to clear the room like Peter, finding a place of solitude and communion with God. In our wired world, this is nearly impossible, and we can see how the enemy of our souls must be gleeful when we live with constant stimuli and noise.

First, find quiet, then kneel. Kneeling is subjugation. It is the way we pay homage to royalty and dignitaries. It is a sign of respect and reverence. To kneel is to say to God that he is God, and we are his people.

Last, we pray. We intercede for the person in need of a miracle. We trust that God can do the miraculous, though we also acknowledge that God's answers do not always align with what we request. So we have faith, but with open hands, leaving the outcomes in his own capable hands.

In this case, God provided a miracle. But God's paradoxical plans do not always involve healing or resurrection in this life. However, we can press on, knowing that everyone who names the name of Jesus will be made completely, utterly whole in the resurrection at the end of time.

> Jesus, I recognize that I can become addicted to noise, music, social media, streaming videos. I can't seem to be alone with my thoughts, not to mention being alone with you. In this moment, I choose quiet. And as I do, I fall to my knees in reverence of who you are and what you have done. Would you hear my prayer today? Amen.

DAY EIGHTY-THREE

PAUL

Ever since I first heard of your strong faith in the Lord Jesus
and your love for God's people everywhere, I have not stopped
thanking God for you. I pray for you constantly, asking God, the
glorious Father of our Lord Jesus Christ, to give you spiritual
wisdom and insight so that you might grow in your knowledge
of God. I pray that your hearts will be flooded with light so
that you can understand the confident hope he has given to
those he called—his holy people who are his rich and glorious
inheritance. I also pray that you will understand the incredible
greatness of God's power for us who believe him.

EPHESIANS 1:15-19

The apostle Paul prays this powerful prayer over the Ephesian believers. His words serve as a model for our prayer lives.

We can thank God for the people in our lives. God has so beautifully peopled our lives with so many individuals. He has woven our relationships into a tapestry of uniqueness, and we can thank him for doing so.

We can pray constantly. At any given moment, we have the privilege of talking to God.

We can trust him as a good Father who loves his children. Ours is not a stodgy deity, angry in the sky. No, he is a Father who cares for us.

We can ask for wisdom and insight as we read his word and endure persecution, trying to live life in this crazy world. We can seek his guidance in our relationships when we cannot find our way. We can ask for help as we navigate budgets, finances, and jobs. He is readily available to give us the insight we need.

We can ask for growth, that we would grow in how deeply we know him. He loves to answer that faith-filled prayer.

We can ask for light to be shed on dark situations and hearts. When we are hopeless, we can ask him for new hope.

We can ask for understanding of our standing in Christ—that we are made holy by his actions on the cross and brought into the family of Christ by the resurrection. We can have victory over darkness because Jesus accomplished that once and for all.

And we who are weak can boldly ask for God's power to be manifested in our weakness.

Jesus, I echo this powerful prayer of Paul's today. I need you. I need your strength. Please grant me the insight and wisdom I need today to follow you well and navigate the world. I pray for growth. Grow me deeply. Root me in your truth. Shed light on what is dark. Lead me forward, dear Jesus. Amen.

DAY EIGHTY-FOUR

PAUL

*I pray that from his glorious, unlimited resources he will
empower you with inner strength through his Spirit. Then
Christ will make his home in your hearts as you trust in him.
Your roots will grow down into God's love and keep you strong.
And may you have the power to understand, as all God's people
should, how wide, how long, how high, and how deep his love
is. May you experience the love of Christ, though it is too great
to understand fully. Then you will be made complete with all
the fullness of life and power that comes from God.*

EPHESIANS 3:16-19

The apostle Paul had a shepherd's heart for the people he met
along the way on his many missionary journeys. Every church
plant weighed heavy upon his heart, and we often see him praying for
each church in his letters. Here he prays for the believers in Ephesus.

There are two ways to apply this prayer—inward and outward.

To look inward, we can pray these amazing blessings for our
own walk with Jesus. It is right and wholly acceptable to ask God for
resources in unlimited forms. After all, the power that raised Jesus from
the dead is the resurrection power living within us through the Holy
Spirit!

We can ask that Christ would grow in our hearts—more of his
loving nature, less of our sinful nature. To make a home is to stay
and dwell, to make a haven for someone. So as we pray that Christ
would dwell in our hearts, we must also pray that we would continue

to make our hearts and souls hospitable places for him: no secrets, less self-interest.

We can ask for roots, deep ones that find the living water. We can ask that we would finally, truly understand the love of Christ poured out upon us. We can ask for completeness—of heart, soul, strength.

To look outward, we can pray all these blessings over a loved one (or even an enemy). We can pray they will experience that same resurrection power. We can ask God to make his home in their hearts, beating strong, giving strength and hope. For those we ache for, we can intercede by seeking and trusting God's steady work in their lives and his ability to root them to him, the rock of their souls. We can ask that God would be to them a refreshing stream in the desert of their current circumstance. In short, we can pray blessing upon them.

No matter how you approach the prayer, inward or outward, the crux is God's amazing ability to empower and help his children. Oh, the resources he brings our way! Oh, the love he pours out on us, though we are undeserving! Oh, what covenantal favor!

Jesus, I pray that you would empower me today to experience your love in a tangible way. I admit, sometimes it's hard for me to understand and grasp it. Would you root me and my loved one to you? Would you shower us with hope today? I pray we would truly find you in the mess of our lives. Amen.

DAY EIGHTY-FIVE

PAUL

I pray that your love will overflow more and more, and that you
will keep on growing in knowledge and understanding. For I
want you to understand what really matters, so that you may
live pure and blameless lives until the day of Christ's return.
May you always be filled with the fruit of your salvation—the
righteous character produced in your life by Jesus Christ—
for this will bring much glory and praise to God.

PHILIPPIANS 1:9-11

The apostle Paul conveys strong affection for the Philippian believers in this prayer. This kind of love is something this world chases after but seldom finds. To pray that people finally grasp their state and their need for a God who saves is the most loving thing we can do.

We can ask for an overflowing love—toward those with whom we spend our days, those whom we struggle to love, and those on the periphery who suffer. To love well is to grow deeper in our understanding of the character of God. There's an intrinsic tie-in—to love is to understand our loving God.

Understanding is important, and Paul's heart here is to see believers truly grasp who they are (children loved by God), what their mission is (to share that love with others), and what their privilege is (to live in a worthy manner before Jesus).

Often throughout the Epistles, Paul mentions the importance of a fruitful life. He prays for the Philippian believers here, asking for fruit. He equates fruitfulness with righteous character—impossible in our own strength, but a strong possibility when we live by the power of the

Spirit within us. To live with good character is to be truly connected to the source of life.

As we live in a connected and fruitful way, we bring Christ glory. Why? Because we ultimately understand that he does the work as we surrender to his ways.

As with yesterday's prayer, we can pray this prayer for ourselves, or we can pray this over our friends, family members, and even those who act as enemies in our lives.

This prayer is particularly poignant when we get to the place in our walk with bitterness where we are finally able to relinquish vengeance and pray blessings like this over those who hurt us. To seek favor on behalf of one who has been bent on harming us is to move from bitterness to hope. To intercede for them and ask for understanding, love poured out, and strength is part of our own healing journey.

> Jesus, I am picturing that person in my life right now who has hurt me. I choose right now to pray for them. Would you help them grow in knowledge and understanding? Would you empower them to live a blameless life? May they be fruitful, longing to bring glory to your name! I surrender my own desire to punish. I replace it with this prayer of blessing. Amen.

DAY EIGHTY-SIX

PAUL

*We have not stopped praying for you since we first heard
about you. We ask God to give you complete knowledge
of his will and to give you spiritual wisdom and
understanding. Then the way you live will always honor
and please the Lord, and your lives will produce every
kind of good fruit. All the while, you will grow as you
learn to know God better and better.*

COLOSSIANS 1:9-10

Paul's prayers are both incessant and intercessory in nature. Prayer
for others is like breathing to him—a constant source of life.
Throughout his epistles, he demonstrates a rigorous prayer life for those
he has shepherded, poured into, and loved. He understands that true
power does not come from personal might, but from a surrendered
heart to the mighty One.

Perhaps you feel like you lack in your prayer life. The solution?
Capture your wayward thoughts by replacing them with prayers—for
yourself, for others, for your day, for strength.

Keeping this continual dialogue with God is not impossible. It's
as simple as turning your attention to him throughout the mundane
moments of your day. When you're perplexed by the problem before
you, pray for insight. When you're upset, pray for understanding.
When someone cuts you off in traffic, pray a blessing over that person.
When you struggle with fear over finances, pray for provision. This
kind of prayer-as-breathing will revolutionize your relationship with
God as he brings you peace throughout your day.

Paul asks directly for spiritual wisdom and understanding—something we all need. When we read the Scriptures, this is an important prayer. We can ask God to open our minds as we pore over difficult portions or ponder larger questions.

Paul's hope for the Colossian believers is that they will grow, produce fruit, and ultimately know God better. How do we grow in a relationship? We spend time together—not just formal moments, but casual ones as well. We laugh together. We seek to know their heart. We talk. We listen. We endure together. We work alongside them. We hope for the future together.

It is similar as we pursue the heart of God. To accomplish this, we simply spend time together—both unstructured and structured. We listen. We talk. We connect. We ask for help. We long to understand his heart. Prayer is the way we can deepen our relationship with God. It is a holy privilege.

Jesus, thank you for this reminder to spend time with you—not just through formal times in church, but also as I walk along, as I fret, as I worry over life. I want to have ears to hear you, eyes to see you in my day. I want to taste and see that you are good. I want to touch you, to experience your touch upon my life. I choose today to pour into our relationship as I would in a relationship with my best friend. Amen.

DAY EIGHTY-SEVEN

PAUL

We keep on praying for you, asking our God to enable you to live
a life worthy of his call. May he give you the power to accomplish
all the good things your faith prompts you to do. Then the name of
our Lord Jesus will be honored because of the way you live, and you
will be honored along with him. This is all made possible because
of the grace of our God and Lord, Jesus Christ.

2 THESSALONIANS 1:11-12

To live worthy of the call of Christ is a weighty matter. After all, Jesus spent his life for us on the cross, and then rose victoriously, conquering death and sin once and for all. He sacrificed all, gave all, relinquished all. If we endeavor to follow a Savior like that, surrender is in order.

Paul hints that the Thessalonian believers are coming to understand the secret of growth—actually walking out their salvation, doing what their faith and the Spirit within them prompt them to do. This is the opposite of quenching the Spirit by disobedience and refusal (see 1 Thessalonians 5:19 ESV).

We honor Christ by our actions. We can boast many things with our mouths, but if we have no actions to back up our boasts, our faith is useless. (See James 2:14-26 for further study.) To speak of our faith and not act accordingly is to live an inauthentic life. But to follow through with the commitments God prompts us to make is to bring honor and glory to him.

This does not mean our actions save us. Only grace, which Paul speaks about here in 2 Thessalonians 1:12, is the reason for our faith.

Our sin separated us from a holy God, and no matter how hard we tried in our strength, we could not atone for our sin. Only a perfect, sinless sacrifice could do such a beautiful work. That sacrifice was Jesus, once and for all. His life, death, and resurrection ushered in the era of grace.

We do not stand on our laurels; we rest on his.

But because we've been given grace so bountifully, we now live our lives in reaction to that grace—and that reaction is action. There is no such thing as passive Christianity. To follow Christ is to pursue him with abandon. It's to get to know him, the power of his resurrection, the fellowship of his suffering (see Philippians 3:10 NKJV). We are given grace, and then we are faced with the great marvel of knowing the One who lavished that grace upon us.

It is a privilege to pray for an active faith—both for ourselves and for those for whom God has prompted us to pray.

Jesus, I pray that I would be so in awe of your grace that I cannot help but follow you in dogged pursuit. I want my actions to reflect what's already in my heart. I am undone by your grace, by your sacrifice on my behalf. You paid the price I could not pay, and you paid it once and for all time. Because of that, I have unfettered access to you. I pray I'll live a grateful, energized life as a result of such greatness. Amen.

DAY EIGHTY-EIGHT

PAUL

I always thank my God when I pray for you, Philemon,
because I keep hearing about your faith in the Lord Jesus
and your love for all of God's people. And I am praying
that you will put into action the generosity that comes
from your faith as you understand and experience all
the good things we have in Christ. Your love has given
me much joy and comfort, my brother, for your kindness
has often refreshed the hearts of God's people.

PHILEMON 4-7

To thank God for another is a beautiful prayer. Sometimes all we can do is simply say, "Thank you." God has so lovingly peopled this earth, and he has woven our web of relationships with intention. We can also augment this prayer by saying it out loud or writing it to another. To look into a friend's eyes and say, "I always thank God for you," is a gift. To write it out in a card is a dignifying act.

As Paul penned this letter, he did so with affection for Philemon. What a powerful way to live—in gratitude for those God has caused to intersect our lives. Note that Paul did not simply write blanket statements about his friend, but he detailed specifics—Philemon's faith, his love for others, his generosity, his comfort, his kindness, the way he lived a life of refreshment toward others. Philemon is special to Paul.

We, too, can encourage others specifically, as Paul has. Even today, we can take a moment to say, text, or handwrite words that will thrill the heart of another. It takes time and intention, but it is not a difficult task. And it may just change the trajectory of someone's day, particularly if we have felt prompted by God to reach out to them.

And we can endeavor, through prayer and the power of the Holy Spirit, to become like Philemon. We can ask God to empower us to exercise more faith, to grow in our love for others, so that we'll be believers of action with generous hearts, able to truly grasp the good things we have in Jesus and to bring those in our lives a constant stream of joy, comfort, kindness, and refreshment.

Oh friend, there are so many riches in knowing Jesus Christ. He gives to us so profoundly, so deeply, so powerfully—yet with gentleness. We cannot mine all of Christ's riches; the more we dig, the more we unearth. To live in gratitude for all he has done is also the language of prayer. To say "Thank you," to live graciously, to throw our hands heavenward in surrender—this is our daily privilege, all because of the greatness of the One who saved us.

Jesus, would you show me someone today whom I can encourage specifically? Would you prompt me to show love to someone who needs to know you see them? Thank you for blessing my life with such amazing folks. I pray you would empower me to be a kindhearted, dedicated friend and family member. I want to live a life of generosity. Amen.

DAY EIGHTY-NINE

ELDERS

*You are worthy, O Lord our God, to receive glory and
honor and power. For you created all things, and they exist
because you created what you pleased.*

REVELATION 4:11

Prayer is not merely asking for situations to improve or people to
change. It can also be a form of worship.

In the posture of prayer, we can meditate on the wonder of God, the
grandeur of his power, the breathtaking beauty of his unfolding plan.

We can mentally walk through the pages of Scripture, noting his
many positive attributes. He is Creator, the fashioner of the stars. He
is the plotter, the Alpha and the Omega, the beginning and the end,
who holds all our stories together in one grand narrative. He is long-
suffering, granting humanity many chances and offering grace throughout our history.

He is a deliverer, taking people from bondage and slavery to free-
dom. He is powerful, able to move walls of water or flood the earth
or rain fire from heaven. He commands the cosmos, names the stars.

He has conquered evil, beginning the process in the garden after
sin infected humanity, then dealing a fatal blow on the cross, crushing
the serpent's head. At the end of time, evil will be vanquished forever,
banished to the lake of fire.

He has empowered people to endure hardship, fire, lions, persecution, sickness, and death. He alighted on people in the form of the

Holy Spirit throughout early history—but after the resurrection of his Son, he graciously granted the Spirit to enliven believers' hearts.

He made a way to have relationship with him by sending his perfect, sinless Son to die on the cross. The hypostatic union—fully God, fully man—became the sacrificial Lamb, once and for all, who died in our place so we could have a place at the table as God's children.

He is the interceding God, who rescued a rebellious humanity on the shoulders of his sacred Son.

He is for us, not against us. He loves us with lavish kindness. He has empowered us with spiritual gifts and fruits. He is within us, without us, beside us, behind us, before us. "In him all things hold together" (Colossians 1:17 ESV). He is all-powerful, all-knowing. He is everywhere. And yet? He is here with us.

God is worthy of our worship.

Jesus, I can scarcely take in just how amazing the Trinity is. Father, Son, Spirit—working in the world to do so many amazing things. You are powerful, strong, empathetic, beautiful. You have stooped to earth to rescue your church. You have sacrificed so I could live. "Thank you" seems far too small. But in this moment today, I choose to worship you for who you are and what you have done. Amen.

DAY NINETY

ANGELS

They sang in a mighty chorus: "Worthy is the Lamb who was
slaughtered—to receive power and riches and wisdom and
strength and honor and glory and blessing."

REVELATION 5:12

Prayer can also involve worshipful singing. Worship will be our primary occupation in heaven, so earth then becomes our practice room for that heavenly joy.

To worship, you must have someone or something to worship. If you worship yourself, your soul will emaciate, because you are a clay-footed creature who cannot enact lasting change on this world. If you worship another person, you face the same predicament. If you worship fame, money, or power, you will eventually be let down.

It is ironic that we end up worshipping the gifts of the only One worthy of worship. We praise riches. We chase wisdom. We long for strength. We scramble for glory. We live for blessing. But all these things come from the One who died on our behalf. We must worship the One who blesses, not the blessings.

Worship involves praising something or someone worthy. And *worthy* is a perfectly apt word to describe God. He who created the world, enacted a plan of redemption, made a people for himself, gave the law and societal norms for a thriving people, broke through creation with the virgin birth, blessed his Son with the purpose of thwarting evil and paying the penalty for sin, taught us how to live in this crazy world with love, brought about crucifixion and glorious resurrection—this is the God we serve. This is the God we worship.

He alone is worthy. He is weighty. He deserves our allegiance. In light of his worth, we find our own. In light of his power, we ask for his. In light of his glory, we bask in his immanent light.

He has carried us thus far in our lives. He bore the weight of our sin upon the tree. He conquered death, rising to life. He has welcomed us into his family, calling us his children. He has given us the gift of the Holy Spirit to be our companion along this journey. He has promised he will never leave us. He will not forsake us.

He is worthy. We choose to humble ourselves before him, praising his goodness, power, and empathy.

This, too, is prayer.

Jesus, I love you. I need you. I worship you who are worthy. You have done so much. You are so much. You are worthy of my life, my surrender, my time, my repentance. May today be a day when I'm constantly aware of your power and beauty. Let worship be on my lips throughout the day. Amen.

NOTES

1. "Genesis 17:18," *Bible Hub*, accessed May 21, 2019, http://biblehub.com/text/genesis/17-18.htm.

2. "H3068—Yehovah—Strong's Hebrew Lexicon (NLT)," *Blue Letter Bible*, accessed May 22, 2019, http://www.blueletterbible.org/lang/lexicon/lexicon.cfm?Strongs=H3068&t=NLT.

3. For a broader look at this idea, see Robert B. Chisholm, "Does God Change His Mind," *DTS Voice*, July 7, 2006, http://voice.dts.edu/article/does-god-change-his-mind-robert-b-chisholm-jr.

4. George Tabac, "Time Elements of the Passover: Type and Antitype," *Herald*, http://www.heraldmag.org/2004/04ma_3.htm, accessed June 18, 2019.

ACKNOWLEDGMENTS

Jesus, thank you for meeting me in the place of prayer. You have revolutionized me, brought me joy. Words fail me to express my deep gratitude.

Thank you to Patrick, as always, for praying alongside me on this journey. I'm grateful for my three adult children, who keep me on my knees. How I love to intercede! Sophie, Aidan, and Julia, you are my joy.

Thanks to those in the Writing Prayer Circle who have prayed me through every book. Thanks go to Kathi, Sandi, Holly, Renee, Caroline, Cheramy, Jeanne, D'Ann, Darren, Dorian, Erin, Helen, Katy G., Katy R., Anita, Diane, Cyndi, Leslie, Liz, Rebecca, Sarah, Tim, Tina, Nicole, Tosca, TJ, Patrick, Jody, Susan, Becky, Dena, Carol, Susie, Cheryl, Christy, Alice, Randy, Paul, Jan, Thomas, Judy, Aldyth, Sue, Brandilyn, Lisa, Richard, Michele, Yanci, Cristin, Roy, Michelle, Ocieanna, Denise, Heidi, Kristin, Sarah, Phyllis, Emilie, Lea Ann, Boz, Patricia, Anna, Kendra, Gina, Ralph, Sophie, Anna, Jodie, Hope, Ellen, Lacy, Tracy, Susie May, Becky, Paula, John, Julie, Dusty, Tabea, Jessica, Cheri, Shelley, Elaine, Ally, and Amy. This has been a particularly difficult year, so your prayers mean so much.

I'm grateful to David and Sarah Van Diest, agents and friends who have encouraged and empowered me.

Thank you, Harvest House, for giving me the platform to share about prayer. To Bob Hawkins Jr., Kathleen Kerr, Sherrie Slopianka, Jessica Ballestrazze, Christianne Debysingh, Ken Lorenz, Betty Fletcher, Brad Moses, Kathy Zemper, Kyler Dougherty, thank you for your hands, hearts, and minds in birthing this book. Thanks, too, for your prayers.

ABOUT THE AUTHOR

Mary DeMuth is a writer, speaker, and podcaster who loves to help people live re-storied lives. Author of more than 40 Christian living books. Mary speaks around the country and the world and is the host of the popular daily podcast *Pray Every Day*, where she prays for you every day of the year. She is the wife of Patrick and the mom of three adult children, currently living in Texas.

Visit Mary at **MaryDeMuth.com**
and be prayed for every day at PrayEveryDay.show

HEALING EVERY DAY

Whatever your circumstance, *Healing Every Day* asks only that you come right where you are to begin a 90-day journey of restoration through the Bible to a healthier, more whole you. As you read Scripture from Genesis to Revelation and allow these devotions to penetrate your heart, you will gain new insights into your past trauma and your hoped-for relief for your present and future joy.

Every day as you say yes to Mary's question *Mind if I pray for you*, you will discover the God who loves you fiercely—right now. He longs to heal your hurting soul. He loves you. He is *for* you. And He's waiting to meet you in all your broken places.

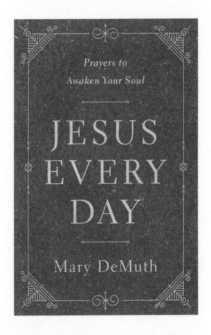

Prayers to
Awaken Your Soul

JESUS EVERY DAY

Mary DeMuth

JESUS EVERY DAY

Trying to juggle all your worries and burdens alone? As the challenges of everyday life threaten to continually distract you, your conversations with God can start to feel threadbare—too rushed to touch on the real issues that crowd your heart.

Rediscover your compassionate Savior with this collection of daily heart-provoking prayers and accompanying Scriptures. Each reading will awaken your tired soul, prompt new ways to encounter Jesus, and inaugurate the kind of authentic conversation you've always yearned to have with Him.

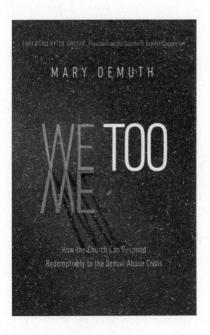

WE TOO

In the throes of the #MeToo movement, Mary DeMuth draws on her personal experience and, with authority and compassion, elevates the voices of survivors as she unpacks the history of the church's response to sexual abuse in order to find a new way forward.

To learn more about Harvest House books and
to read sample chapters, visit our website:

www.harvesthousepublishers.com

HARVEST HOUSE PUBLISHERS
EUGENE, OREGON